Praise for som
Hugh Prather's other books:

"*How to Live in the World and Still Be Happy* offers more than hope. It is a lifeline. Thank you, Hugh! You surely opened my eyes . . . again!"

    —**IYANLA VANZANT**, author of *Yesterday, I Cried* and *One Day My Soul Just Opened Up*

"*How to Live in the World and Still Be Happy* will set your soul dancing. Thank you, Hugh, for another treasury of lightness and love."

    —**NEALE DONALD WALSCH**, author of *Conversations with God*

"Hugh Prather has distilled a treasure trove of practical, spiritual wisdom in *The Little Book of Letting Go.*"

    —**JOAN BORYSENKO**, Ph.D., author of *Minding the Body, Mending the Mind* and *A Woman's Journey to God*

"Learning to let go is one of the greatest gifts you can give yourself and share with others."

    —**RICHARD CARLSON**, author of *Don't Sweat the Small Stuff*

Shining Through

Also by Hugh Prather

How to Live in the World and Still Be Happy

The Little Book of Letting Go

Standing on My Head

Love and Courage

Notes to Myself

*Spiritual Notes to Myself: Essential Wisdom
for the 21st Century*

*I Will Never Leave You: How Couples Can Achieve
the Power of Lasting Love*

a 30-day program

Shining Through

Switch On Your Life and Ground Yourself in Happiness

HUGH PRATHER

CONARI PRESS

First published in 2004 by Conari Press,
an imprint of Red Wheel/Weiser, LLC
York Beach, ME
With offices at:
368 Congress Street
Boston, MA 02210
www.redwheelweiser.com

Library of Congress Cataloging-in-Publication Data
Prather, Hugh.
   Shining through : switch on your life and ground yourself in
   happiness / Hugh Prather.
      p.   cm.
   ISBN 1-57324-954-8
      1. Conduct of life. 2. Happiness. I. Title.
   BJ1581.2.P44 2004
   170'.44—dc22   2004010736

Typeset in Berkeley Oldstyle, Suburban, and Triplex by Suzanne Albertson
Printed in Canada
TCP

 11 10 09 08 07 06 05 04
  8 7 6 5 4 3 2 1

Contents

Contents

Contents

Contents

Contents

Stories and Experience

The world tells many stories. So often they begin in hope and end with despair. Unquestionably there are sorrow and suffering in the world, often more than it seems we can bear. But there is another story, one that has already begun and will not end. It springs from absolute beauty, yet frequently it cannot be seen within the events of the world. It is what might be called the Divine Ballad, an ancient song held within every heart. It can bring peace to any mind; its lyrical grace and gentle reassurance can be experienced by anyone. It is God's gift, your inheritance and mine. And it can never be lost or forfeited.

In this book, I attempt to present a few ways our mind can begin to hear the song of our heart and experience a growing faith in the Truth that exists beyond our tragedies and fears. Clearly, abiding comfort and wholeness cannot be based on what always changes. It is vital to find an approach that permits us to experience a reality greater and more reliable than the confusing and surprisingly short journey of our body. I will suggest ways this might be done. I have tried to make them direct and simple enough to promote experiences that ignite hope—because hope can allow eyes long closed to beauty to finally open.

Fear and conflict are misdirections that create mental turmoil within so many of us. They are ways of not focusing, of not being whole. They keep the mind in a state of vulnerability that in turn makes the terrain of our life very hard and quite frightening. There are times when we don't even know what we are afraid of. We avoid something we are not even sure is there. Stillness dispels fear and conflict by restoring our willingness to look beyond the mere surface of individuals and events. Through either direct or gradual means, the thoughts and exercises in this book will urge you to look, to be honest, to be still, so that the grounds for happiness can be clearly seen.

And these grounds will never be comparative. True gratitude is not based on the perception that others have less or suffer more. It is the recognition that love rather than apprehension holds lasting value, and that there is no end to the embrace of love. Because love does exist, you and I can be free.

Hugh Prather
November 16, 2003
Tucson, Arizona

Assumptions of This Book

There are two levels of perception. The first is like a dream, full of conflict and shifting emotions, victories won and lost. The second reflects Love and brings with it a sense of eternity and changelessness. We can always tell which of these perceptions we are using by how we feel. For even though there may be occasions when we like a dream, we sense the mindset of anxiety from which it rises. In contrast, when we perceive accurately, we begin to feel a deep and freeing peace and a certainty about the outcome of all things.

At the start of our journey, the perception of love may appear to come and then quickly go. And for many of us there will be long periods of comparative bleakness. Yet beneath it all will be a growing sense of innocence and a deepening conviction that a Friend walks beside us and holds our hand in gentleness. It eventually becomes clear that we have not been abandoned by Reality but only chose to look away a while. All of us experience tragedies in our lives; some of us, of course, far more devastating ones than others. Yet we all know fear and loss. We also experience triumph and joy. The world seems at times perilous and, at times, a place of hope. But the one thing it can never give us is constancy, and because of this we feel that we must never let down our guard, never relax into certainty. The world requires constant vigilance.

Regardless of how we perceive our life, nothing external can deprive us of our Home. If the world is constantly changing, there is still one Place of rest and beauty that remains unchanged, always present and ever with us.

What then must we do to wake to the recognition that Reality has never changed? We need merely open our eyes. Instead of beginning still another useless search for small advantages, we must look honestly at the nature of what continually shifts, for it can never give us what we long for—a real Home that cannot be destroyed, lost, or even betrayed. In place of a chaotic vision, we must choose Love, not only because it is fair to all but because it is a simple fact, and the only one there is.

To recognize Love as real is never again to desire a compromise decision. We turn from a world of conflict—from all it seemed to hold out to us but never relinquished, and from all it appeared to do to us that we have not sufficiently avenged. We withdraw from that useless, endless fight and accept freedom instead. We turn and face the Light. No more than this. And if we find we have not freed ourselves completely, we practice a while longer only what will make a difference: Charity without identification with pain. Gentleness that is strong and consistent. And happiness that is not snatched and is not hidden.

Each time we practice love, we open our eyes a little further on the Place of Love. Love is our means and our end. It is our Home, our Family, and our Identity. That evidence, seen and felt, reveals the emptiness of dreams. But if we treat the means of our awakening as a trinket, something merely to be worn occasionally like some clever adornment, it will have no deep meaning for us and cannot disclose its limitless worth.

Perhaps waking to Love seems impractical. There is always so much to do, so many things to consider. Perhaps it seems insensitive in the face of tragedy and evil, or too pessimistic in light of the beauty and grandeur that also characterize the world. There are innumerable reasons not to have faith in another Reality. But if we dwell on them, we cannot experience the freedom and joy of a Peace that is not dependent on external events, because now our happiness is contingent on the future, and the future will not be controlled.

It is easy to argue against a Truth that does not separate one from another, a God who does not seek vengeance. The world we live in has been making this argument for many long years, and just looking around at ordinary life seems to prove the point. Many have sought to make God a huge irritated infant, a super ego who sits above us playing with a magic wand. We hope It hates our enemies, yet we imagine that It capriciously punishes or rewards both the wicked and the good. But in the stillness of our heart we know this perception is not accurate.

We also know that God is not contained in a particular religion or system of beliefs. We know that even the attempt to define the Divine is as futile as trying to capture the beauty of a butterfly by pinning it to a display board. This book does not seek to explain the world or to teach anyone how to make it work. Rather, it is an attempt to write in various and alternative ways about the peace of God, which is merely a term and cannot begin to express the magnitude and splendor of the Stillness that surrounds and fills us all.

It is time to put aside our ways of being right and bask together in the Love that comforts all creatures great and small. Pull your decision to walk straight into God around every part of you and over every instant of your day and night. Exclude no one and no thing. Make it the thought you wake with and the goal you cherish in your sleep. See no other person without light, and light will begin to pervade each crack and corner of your surroundings, until you recognize that you have never left the Place where Love watches over you who are the child, the meaning, and the joy of God.

Essays of Encouragement

Potential

Your potential as a healer is limitless. Is it not true that you have something of value to offer? Haven't you seen some evidence in your life of your potential to give a gift that will gladden the heart of someone else? Haven't you been kind? Haven't you uplifted? Haven't you helped someone at some time not to feel isolated and misunderstood? And is that potential in you not worth your effort to release more fully, and consistently? Your potential is love. And love is of God. To make others happy will do far more than make you happy. It will begin to release the world from pain and turn hell into Heaven.

Wisdom

This is the lesson; this is all that is being learned: Forgiveness truly is the key to happiness, to simple liking, to heartfelt contentment, to the enjoyment of other people, to remaining present, and to the certainty that we already exist in freedom. Just forgive, merely relax and let go of dislikes and justified resentments, simply forget grievances and bleak anticipations, just set all things free of dark memories and cruel expectations. Let loose, let go, let be, and the earth cannot help but sing and your heart dance with it. Forgive and be happy. That is the ancient secret, the inner teaching, the hidden answer, the lost knowledge, the message of the still, quiet voice, and the only wisdom ever to be attained.

Control

I turn from what I cannot improve to what I can. If I can't heal my body, I *can* heal my mind and thus free myself to make peaceful decisions. I alone choose what preoccupies me. Thought can be turned to either chaos or stillness. I can choose not to endlessly trace the "causes" of my difficulties and project onto the future their limitations and pains. If I can't make certain people stop condemning me, I can stop analyzing their motives and rest from defending my actions. No matter what appearances I dislike or fear, I *can* turn away from my wearying attempts to tinker them into perfection.

Let me begin with what can be changed this instant. My mind can open to the stillness of God. And within its soft appeal, what cannot be seen with peace? Or at least seen with the faith that if I could look through God's eyes, I might understand that even this before me now will dissolve in Love's embrace.

Love

The only Reality that can unite the little creatures and the large, all people, plants, and pets, all purposes, needs, and potentials, is Love. In Love's gentle arms, the fractured pieces are healed and made whole. Every lost hope, every field of grass come and gone, every song ended, every life wasted, every sun swallowed by darkness is resurrected and restored, is kept and cherished, and is forever here, in me, in everyone, in peace. And what must I do to experience this bounty? Merely be kind. Kind in my thoughts and gestures. Kind in the way I see and hear. Kind to my body and spirit. Kind even to my ego. For what is like Love is within Love. Simply be kind, and the Kingdom of all kingdoms surrounds me.

Release

Today I will allow all things to be as they are. I will judge nothing. I am willing for the weather to be whatever it is. I am content to take part in each encounter that is to come, experiencing without resistance the circumstances in which I am placed. I will let my friends act however they will. I will release my attention from censure to rest on this gentle moment. I will allow the members of my family to be what they are, without *defining* what they are. I will attempt to see my children as they are, without interpretations drawn from my experience and free of motivations I have attributed to them. I will not assign my partner's role or function or attitude toward me. I will not cherish a wish for a shift in personality or habits, nor will I try to push anyone in a particular direction by moderating my joy or withholding my normal responses. I will let all people be just as they are today. And within the stillness this brings, I will ask how the Divine is able to love each one, a love so intimate that we are transformed into the children of God.

Fantasizing

What has a reasonable chance of giving me simple happiness within this instant? Imagining future arms of flesh, or visualizing the present and willing arms of Love? Fantasizing future riches, or pausing to sense the deep and endless wealth of my Core? Planning little triumphs over others, or sensing what caring and delight could pass between me and some living thing? Isn't one kind use of my mind a more practical act than a thousand vain imaginings? Why do I fill my thoughts with scenes and plans that, even if they occurred, would not make me feel complete or even gratify me for more than a little while, when I could spend this very moment attempting something restful and peaceful and lastingly enjoyable? When will I accept the soft truth of today and recognize the uselessness of my thoughts about tomorrow?

Disguises

We often hurt ourselves as a means of teaching ourselves "lessons." We lecture our minds, discipline our
bodies, and writhe in guilt. We make rigid rules about
how we must behave, impose unkind boundaries on
our relationships, and prejudge our use of time. That
is why we find it difficult to believe there is Something
that does not use pain as a teaching aid. That is also
why we are suspicious of the motives of others. Yet
this suspicion must at least be *questioned* if we are ever
to allow ourselves to feel the quiet presence of the
Divine. There is indeed a Hand held out to us in love.
It will never be withdrawn. We have been assured of
this more than once. Why would the Creator need
"trials" to determine the quality of creation? Why
would God need to "test" the nature of our soul? The
Universe simply does not have anything up its sleeve.
And the Divine does not slap our hands to teach us
love.

Thinking

Mind cannot think outside of mind. Thoughts can't separate themselves from the one who thinks them. That is why I will never succeed in dismissing other people. If I have a thought about them, they are within me; they are "mine." What then do I wish to make of this piece of my mind? A garden or a slaughterhouse? My mind holds everything in a vast circle of pure spirit. I cannot think a disturbing thought without requesting that everything share in my distress. Nor can I be at peace without offering peace to the entire world that peoples my thought. Because listening is love, love can be transmitted through silence as easily as through pronouncements and deeds. And because minds have no boundaries, I can't have a thought that is no one else's business. Petty thoughts may have only temporary effects, but without love, there are no lasting gestures, and no real communication has actually taken place.

Beginning

If I am unwilling to let this problem go completely, let me at least loosen my grip a little. I will create some softness around the edges by stepping aside and waiting a moment for another point of view to come to me. I will allow a small measure of stillness into my mind. At least I will let my mind consider a moment's rest, if not a happy laugh of relief. Love itself is what calls to me to give myself comfort. It is *not* humble to remain in turmoil, and Love does not ask this of me. I will reach for one peaceful thought. And I will feel God's support of this endeavor. Something has begun if I make no more than a single effort in the present. Starting over takes less time than analyzing why I have stopped.

Knowing

It is by refusing to make decisions about my life, any decision at all, that I can open my mind to quiet correction and gentle instruction. I must be firm in my knowledge that I don't know anything. This is the one thing I do know. Whatever about me is justified and "right" holds little hope. Truth is perfect Wholeness, but I cannot claim to be perfectly whole. That means that what I think I know is at best incomplete. Rather than use time to weigh what I should do, it is far better for me to take time to remember that no circumstance exists for me to decipher, no individual lives about whom I must decide. If I look back on what I once considered my victories and defeats, it is clear that I am not even in a position to calculate my own improvement. Therefore, let me be still and patiently await Love's knowing. It will do more than just direct me. To hear God's call is to be literally encompassed in gentleness. The place described in my heart is the Place. To hear it spoken of is to be included in It within the same instant. What is of God is God.

Interpreting

Because nothing I see holds a solitary, permanent meaning, I am free to give it the meaning I wish. I don't have to strive for the right interpretation because there simply is none. The question is how do I *want* to interpret what another person has said, what an event means, what a physical symptom symbolizes. And will I understand that the meaning I assign is merely a preference? If I question the validity of my personal tastes and judgments, my first reaction to another's behavior is also called into question. A given tone of voice, a particular set of the face or body, the use of certain words, can now be whatever I choose to hear and see. The day is my coloring book. So let a fresh rendering form in my mind. Let me freely use the deeper tones of peace and compassion. The world I see is not immovable, and I am not insane to deny its dark traditions. If, in the beginning, I do not feel the substance of my new perception, I will begin by softly singing the echoes of Truth deep within me and project my voice onto the world.

Vision

What I see with my body's eyes is not all that is there. What I see with love is also real. As a lampshade surrounds a light, so bodies appear to encircle spirit and words imprison thought. But there is always more occurring than the appearance of limitation. Spirit is invisible to eyes and cannot be heard with ears alone, yet sounds and objects begin to brighten as I focus my spiritual senses. I simply say "I bless you" to everything, and if I mean it, words crack open with new life, and all the gauzy lampshades on earth begin to vanish before a world of immeasurable beauty and light. When I extend kindness to the people and things around me, I extend my vision and understanding as well. And when I am consistently kind to myself, I not only see myself as whole, I also become whole.

Mind

Objects are seen through eyes, not with eyes. Whereas Reality is seen with love, not through it. This is because only a mind experiences sight, and only a mind contains love. No one has to earn their mind, but they do have to use it. To ask "What am I doing with my mind?" is to question everything that needs to be questioned. When I am *truly* thinking, Love is the mind with which I think. It gathers together the scattered pieces of my consciousness and makes whole the devastation of my life. Is the thought I am now entertaining a thought of connection or separation? Is it leading to an experience of understanding and equality? Or am I disconnecting from someone or from myself? And just how far do I want to take this? The more defensive I become and the more I make demands, the less I truly use my mind. Shattered and blind, I pity myself mightily and claim not the wholeness of Mind I never lost.

Praying

We do not speak into the heavens or even into another's ears. On that level nothing meaningful is said or heard. We can't get the attention of the Divine; we already have it. To be of real help to ourselves or another, we must speak into the place of Beauty. It is a place encircled by holiness and filled with the soft atmosphere of peace. We speak quietly into Stillness. Peacefully, we extend pure peace. There is some place where our voice will extend today. This is inevitable. It can be a place without light and hope or one with promise of abiding comfort. What we must listen for before we speak is a softening of our heart and a sweetening of our mind. This allows the gentle tide of Love to move quietly through us out into the world, and back into our soul.

Desires

If I know what the results will be, even if only intellectually, why continue to be dishonest with myself? If all external pursuits eventually lead to distress, then I have not in truth discovered an exception *this* time. Whenever I notice a lower impulse, any equivocal motivation, I will remind myself quickly that my ego can never take me to a place I would really want to be. Yearnings for future blessings are merely denials made in the present. Acquisitions, indulgences, and small reprisals are not desirable if I am already whole. I don't need to know the "right" people or be in the "right" places. There are none. I don't need to take my body back in time, for that is impossible. Nor will I achieve a degree of contentment from withdrawal and cynicism. If I know this sorry self-image will never be successfully enhanced, why try? The ego can't be perfected. But the attempt to do so is not without consequence. We become ensnarled in ceaseless war. Have we not been told that we are one Self, created of Love, a perfect song in Heaven, a child of Light loved without limit, an indistinguishable part of Everything? The only time that can be remembered is this instant.

Rest

The Answer comes in only one size yet fits all problems. Most difficulties are equally easy or hard to solve. They are either all easy or all difficult, depending on my willingness to relax my mind. Difficulty is inherent in any situation. Our path is a path of problems. Yet no one experiences constant hardship. At times a classically tormenting circumstance is dealt with peacefully; at other times one small annoyance can be overwhelming. Mental softness and flexibility mark the difference, and nothing softens the mind like love. Kindness is the great emollient. Why then are we not relieved to know that all Love wants is for us to be tolerant, that all Peace wants is for us to be happy? Is this a demand or a gift? Love cannot soften my response if I insist on taking advantage of every opportunity to be miserable. The Divine presence is like gentle water washing over rocks. It lifts me above the hard things if I am willing to float. Relax, my little mind, for God is here. Lean on the forever Harmless. Faith is simply rest.

Miracles

Love works miracles. Yet what do I choose to emphasize—the miracle or the Love it reflects? If I shift my attention to the miracle, I lose sight of its Cause. What is important is important, and what is symbolic is not deserving of preoccupation. If its source is God, the only true miracle is one that blesses anyone and everyone. If the miracle makes no sense to a political prisoner or a member of a lost tribe, then it is merely an empty form that at best represents someone's fantasy of personal gain. God is indeed our Friend, but only human friends play favorites. For me friendship is measured in camaraderie and reciprocity, but how could the sun withhold luster from a single leaf, and how could the Divine fail to kiss the forehead of any child? The Parent of us all does not write us out of the will of God, and no matter how far I walk toward hell, Love walks before me.

Being Right

Have I just composed the rules for my happiness? Have I set the conditions and described the necessary course of events that this day must provide? If I have told myself how long this task or errand should take and how things should appear when completed, I have set my own trap. If I fail to pass the test—which I surely will—I will store another small shame in the attic of my mind and add to my hoard of pious pity. I can prove that I am right by being unhappy, or I can be happy by giving up being right. Between wrong and right is a soft nest into which I can settle. From this vantage point, like watching clouds drift toward me, I can let events come to me. I can free myself and this day from measurements and demands and wish all living things well.

Guilt

Guilt is a useful emotion if it reminds me of the times I have hurt others and makes me feel again a deserved self-contempt. To wince at the memory of betrayal is a purifying pain. But to wallow in my guilt fixes my mind on a mistake instead of on its correction. The purpose of seeing how I don't want to act is to act otherwise. If our mind is a channel for Love, it is either open or closed to Love's yearning to reach out through us and make others happy. Preoccupation with guilt keeps it closed and so perpetuates the original love-less error. Do I, in fact, honor my God? Then let me stop interfering so that the Parent of us all may show through me how unfailing and ceaseless is Love. Guilt as self-indulgence is a lack of respect for the Divine and cannot heal anything.

Lines of Thought

From my stillness and from my conflict arise many guides, but which I choose to follow is my responsibility. Today I will make a consistent attempt to follow the leadings of wholeness and peace. I will not give my mind over to the assumption that some parts of chaos make sense, while certain aspects of Oneness can be ignored. Instead, I will think, recall, anticipate, and reason along lines marked by fairness and illuminated in freedom. Today I will not deceive myself that thoughts are idle. I will gently watch over my mind to keep it an enjoyable source of experience, and I will use it in ways that will honor me by honoring the Origin of my being.

Purposes

I always assign some purpose to my use of time. I am never without motive. What can be changed is the source from which the purpose comes. If there is conflict in the part of me I draw on to give meaning to what I do, then I assign an ever-changing and scattered series of small goals to disconnected and themeless moments, and my day jumps from one petty intention to another. But if I draw from my quiet heart, from my still and unified self, a single purpose bridges time, and I recognize the interests of all living things as the same. When purpose is whole within me, I have no intentions that could not be shared by anyone. What, then, is this moment *for*? Let me not be afraid to ask.

Time

What is the purpose of time? Is it to be happy? Is it to feel oneness with another? I can get excited thinking of what may come, but not entirely comfortable. The future is a road of uncertainty, and even an overwhelming anticipation is undercut by basic honesty. No one knows the future; it is not held in our hands. Nor can past accomplishments or pleasantries bring complete peace. They are over and done with, and just how they relate to the present is anyone's opinion. There is no better time than now. Unless I pull thoughts of what was or what might be into it, now alone is free of fear and longing. All events are time-oriented, yet it is possible to allow each event to come to me in its own time. All thoughts are shaped by the future and the past, yet it is possible to think from stillness, to center the source of my thoughts in peace. But there is no peace in yearning for times that no longer exist or anticipating a life that has not begun. God is within the present, as is my heart. Now is the sacred meeting ground.

Gifts

The little breaks I take from pain, my periods of rest and quiet meditation, are gifts I give myself and everyone I have ever known. I am only doing the enjoyable, nothing more. My wish is simply to think thoughts that make me happy and to rest from those that are barren of love. If in my mind you are damaged, an image broken or alone, I bestow peace upon myself as well as on you when I see you once again as you are, held forever perfect in the heart of Beauty. Let me then imagine an entire world I would truly like to be part of, because my effort is serving to bring it about. Let me remember that it is not my duty to pray, it is my fond pleasure.

Resolve

I will not begin again until I can feel the strength in my resolve. I will not start halfheartedly. For the rest of this day my goal is a quantitative one. I will make a new effort to bring more aspects of my life to sanity than I have ever done before. I will renew my purpose frequently, and I will remind myself that whenever I allow my goal to be the same as God's, it cannot fail. I *will* try harder today; that much at least is within my control. I will try for release of irritation and cold resistance. I will try for simple understanding, for an even-handed and gentle vision. I will try for a day of continuing peace and effortless doing, that my mind may extend a blanket of quietness over every place and situation I see. And should my heart again become angry or unyielding, as quickly as possible I will return to Love's way and my true will.

Grievances

I release you from my hurt feelings. I free you from my reading of your motives. I withdraw my "justified" outrage and leave you clean and happy in my mind. In place of censure, I offer you all of God's deep contentment and peace. I will perceive you singing, with a soft smile of freedom and a glow of rich satisfaction. I bless you my brother, my sister. You are a shining member of the Family of God, and I will wait patiently for this truthful vision to come honestly to my mind.

Listening

I give this time to You alone. Please guide me in this prayer. I ask only that I be honest with myself and honest with You. May I pray from my heart alone. If there is anything I should experience now, or any thought I should notice, I am ready to receive it. In stillness and quiet listening, I now open myself to You.

Emptiness

Now I lay down the past hour and the past days. Many times I have forgotten what is important and have lifted what is unimportant to a position of prominence in my mind. But regretting that is not my purpose now. I release myself from all thoughts of guilt and failing. I let all witnesses to instability and weakness be still. Empty of the past, I turn to You. I know nothing now, not even about myself. Fill me completely with your Heart.

Bleakness

These thoughts will not go away, so I pause now and once again turn them over to You. I have been asking for peace, yet I am clearly not at peace. You have said that all I need do is ask sincerely. Don't my efforts alone show that I am sincere in wanting to let go of this bleakness and see instead your Beauty? There seems to be some catch in all of this. If willingness is all that is needed, haven't I already done my part many times over? I have been still; I have asked; I have meditated; and the distress continues. I have tried to listen for instruction and have heard nothing. I am exhausted in both doing and not doing. So I fail. I fail in You. I give up completely. I stumble and fall into You.

No Exceptions

I want to see You everywhere so that in all honesty I may be at peace with what I see. That my mind may be a place of rest, I want You to be a part of each consideration, every wish, memory, and meaning. I will affirm no habit that is not fair, no rule of conduct that cannot set free, no emotion that does not embrace in honor or enfold in safety and peace. Seen wherever I look, acknowledged wherever my thought turns, heard in every remark and any sound at all, be You my universe, my one Self, my All.

Complete

You are the breath that inspires me,
The water that purifies me,
The food that nourishes and gratifies.
Yours is the Mind with which I pray,
And Yours the Life by which I live.
I offer Your thoughts in love,
For Your peace leads me to heal.
You open wide my eyes and guide my feet.
You still my anxious heart.
You are my Love, my Father, my Mother,
And my Self.
I recognize all others in your Face.
You are the Friend in all my friends,
My one Relationship.
You are my rest, my Home, and my Identity.
You are but all there is.
I am complete in You.

A Thirty-Day
Course

Affirmation

Because God is with me, I am content
to be wherever I am.

Guide

Anytime I feel distress today, I will remind myself that
it is no accident that I am wherever I am. And I am
glad to be here, because within this place and instant,
God holds my hand in love. Anytime I feel a twinge
of longing, I will ask myself if it is likely that God is
unaware of my needs. And I will lean on the Divine
and return my mind to trust.

Affirmation
What do I want this to mean?

Guide

Today I will practice letting go of my first reaction and allowing my second reaction to come from love. If something does not please me, I will be still an instant and gently question the meaning I have given it. Rather than interpreting or reinterpreting, I will listen instead for a meaning as peaceful as God's.

Affirmation

All released . . . all is peace.

Guide

As I release everything from darkening recollections and visions of uncaring "laws," I behold all living things at peace and completely safe in God's care. Today's affirmation can be used in rhythm with breathing. Or I can picture its meaning everywhere as a means of calming my mind. And it is indeed a proper blessing for anyone I am tempted to condemn. I release my darkness, and my gift is light.

Affirmation

Guilt is the same mistake in another form.
To bless is my decision.

Guide

No one has ever been helped by being judged. Nor can thoughts of guilt heal the ones I have injured. If I have made a mistake, let me correct it now, at least within my own mind. Today my response to any mistake I recognize will be to offer healing and a deep inner blessing rather than using my mind self-indulgently, for embarrassment and shame are still all about me.

Affirmation

My body is a means of communicating love.

Guide

The ego often uses the body to make others feel separate. Love uses it to make them happy. I will begin with the times I recognize that I am putting my body to some use and quietly examine my motive. If it is not to extend peace and enjoyment, I will acknowledge how small and anxious a thing I have become in my own eyes, and I will pick instead some gentle emotion to let my body pass along.

Affirmation

To gain the position of freedom, I will step
back to the position of love.

Guide

In the various situations that arise today, my ego will
offer me two options: winning or losing. God will offer
me a third: equality. Competitiveness is a request for
pain because it questions the fairness of God's love, in
which no one is slighted. Within equality is freedom,
for in true equality limits are renounced for everyone.
Today I will reject a position of advantage so I may
practice a position of peace.

Affirmation

I will let no idle thought continue unreleased.

Guide

The ego mind is like a stream of agitated fish. Today I will not go fishing. Most idle thoughts contain elements of attack, but they cannot harm me or anyone unless I snatch them from the pointless and make their meanspiritedness my own. I entertain thoughts of connection, or I hold on to ones devoid of it. That choice will be my preoccupation today, for it alone determines my experience.

Affirmation

If I choose peace, I will not be at peace alone.

Guide

Nor can I choose fear alone. Every mind is linked, and what I cannot help but pass along is not my private affair. I will pause long enough today to let this fact have its effect on my mindset and mood. Each time I decide for comfort, let me picture someone else relaxing at this same instant. And when I choose to indulge my self-righteousness or my self-pity, let me see also the blessing I fail to confer.

Affirmation
I will pause often for instruction today.

Guide
There is no step so small that I would not improve my chances for happiness by listening an instant before I proceed. There is a reason why God has given us a quiet place within our hearts, and there is a gentle logic to noticing our peaceful preferences.

Affirmation
Let my first step be stillness.

Guide

How can I expect Love's interpretation to enter a mind that loudly insists on another view? How can I feel God's deep peace while I angrily judge everything around me? No matter what the source of my complaint, or from what direction affliction seems to come, my inward reaction today will be gently to do nothing. The Divine in me is very still; the ego is very restless; therefore I will choose the way of peace.

Affirmation
Learning to respond to now
is all there is to learn.

Guide

Each instant I remember, I will take a closer look at this present moment and all it contains. The journey to God is the journey into now. To ascend into Heaven is to sink so deeply into now that I lose all interest to the past and future. The ego was and will be, but only God is.

Affirmation
Today there is nothing to decide.

Guide

Because there is a Plan, nothing remains to be decided. The answer has been given, my way set, and my Guide provided. A thousand times today, I will fall back into the arms of God. And if any question arises, I will simply say, "You decide," and know that it is done.

Affirmation

Help is not being forced on me.

Guide

Help lies gently on my mind, waiting only for my invitation to enter. We are not coerced or tricked into Heaven. Every step I take is at my bidding, and my decision to be good or to be destructive is my responsibility. Happiness is the choice I must make, and fear the only sacrifice. To any sign of resistance I will say, "Help is not being forced on me."

Affirmation

My will is not threatened by God's.
To feel Love's impulse is to recognize my own.

Guide

God knows what I will enjoy. It is not Love's plan to hurt or deprive anyone. Can I see all possible ramifications of the least of my idle wishes? Then let me not presume a conflict that does not exist. It is the pleasure of Love to carry us through the lawns of Heaven and to set us down by the quiet waters of Peace. Instead of trusting uninformed imaginings, I will practice listening to my stillness today, knowing it tells me of God's will and of my own.

Affirmation
I will make no effort to step ahead of God.

Guide
If the ocean were pure mind and I were a wave, I would be in terror if I tried to distinguish myself from the water that produced me. What is a wave without water, and what is a mind without God? My ego searches for ways to set itself apart from others and become "self"-sufficient. But today I will be still and acknowledge that I am where You are and what You are.

Affirmation

If I desire any change in the surface,
I cannot see beyond it.

Guide

My body's eyes show me the surface of things, yet Love looks past form into pure content. To choose to do whatever I am doing, and to choose not to hold other people's behavior against them, is to decide to see. Every time I take up arms today against appearances, I will remember that my sight is improved by laying them down.

Affirmation

All power and glory lie within my
harmlessness, which is of God.

Guide

My practice today will take one simple direction: *I will
hurt no one in my thought or in my life.* Let me be honest
in this and also in assessing its effects.

Affirmation
Let me at least try.

Guide

God has not withheld any answers, and if I will look within my mind, I will recognize at least one or two small steps I can take immediately. My need is not for mastery but merely for the willingness to practice an instant more. A small step toward light is better than total darkness. This day is not lost if there is still one moment left in which to begin again.

Affirmation

I will not use my mind to
build a case against freedom.

Guide

I will not follow up on thoughts of limitation and
frailty, suffering and death. I can unite with my stricken
sisters and brothers without confining my mind to suffering. Today I will not pursue any perception that
would delay my return to You. For it is our return
Home that also releases the world.

Affirmation

Gentleness of thought is my way Home.

Guide

Do I want to take time to justify my position, or can I lay aside shows of dignity and demands for respect as unnecessary delays? Today I will stop to ask myself if I am ready to be happy on the spot, or must I insist on handling my self-image first. Acknowledged equality quiets the mind. Spiritual advancement is merely choosing to be still.

Affirmation

I will quietly extend whatever I appear to lack.

Guide

Any emptiness or lack or sense of longing I may feel today will indicate the precise gift for me to give to others. I will reach out my thoughts to fill and embrace the hearts of those who come to mind. With a deep and satisfying gift from God's storehouse, I will extend my blessing, thus proving I am blessed.

Affirmation

Give what I would have; see what I would be.

Guide

Within time, I must first give to receive, and see in others what I would recognize as my Self. All I have to give is an innocent vision, yet to give this much is to bestow Heaven itself. Today I will practice in front of God's mirror, and I will honor Beauty in the face of every child of Love.

Affirmation
Today I will not project.

Guide

My attitude characterizes what I see, but it is possible to see without attitude. Insight is marked by stillness, and projection is marked by excitement or dislike. When I add a version of myself to individuals and places, the quietness goes out of my perception. Now what I see is what I have decided to see and not what might be changing before my very eyes. Just as is true of dogs and insects, some people's egos are more destructive than others', and this can be honestly perceived. But when I add judgment to the seeing, my insight is locked in time. Thus no two egos view an individual in the same way. Once I understand this, I am free to seek the one and infinite Interpretation. I will know I have done this when once again I can see the gentle Transformation that works within all.

Affirmation

All correction begins and ends in me.

Guide

Let me recognize the times today that I can profit from this reminder. I am not charged with obtaining someone's cooperation or removal or any other change in outward circumstances. I am the sole and proper object of my efforts to correct. My mental state will, of itself, extend to all those I hold in thought. That is why only my mental state needs healing.

Affirmation

God is the power by which I rule my mind.

Guide

My freedom and release are attainable because my mind is subject to my will. It focuses where I instruct and reacts as I command. And a mind focused on God is wholly within Love. Today I choose to look for peace, forbearance, goodwill, and signs of enjoyment, that I may begin to see What surrounds me.

Affirmation

I will not rehearse uncertainties to come.

Guide

As best I can, I will fear no evil fortune and imagine no gathering storm. Worry is not intuitive, and fears are not the messengers of God. I am not protected by always looking over my shoulder or guessing the form of every shadow I see. Instead, I will ask Love what it is I need to do and trust the details of the Answer.

Affirmation
My mind is cradled in the peace of God.

Guide
Because Your blessing encircles it and flows softly through it, my heart beats gently. My eyes and ears are comforted by Your loving presence. My feet walk in Beauty, a path of peace prepared by You, and my hand holds Yours in Oneness. I am Your child brought safely Home.

Affirmation

The Self that I am is God's alone.

———————————

Guide

God is not a bigger ego to which I must submit. The yearnings for good I feel deep within me are God's very Voice and my own will. There are no separate identities in Oneness. God's Love is my love. God's Vision shows me my reality. Let me treat as sacred the I that I am and see no limits or competitions within my Self. Where could the I that I am end and the I that is God begin, if All is One in Love?

Affirmation

All is still. All is quiet. All is God.

Guide

Behind these words is the only experience that will satisfy me. Whatever troubles me, I can sing these words silently, deeply, and slowly in my heart. And I can safely believe that this Truth exists within the core of everyone I encounter or have ever known. You have not left me. Nor is any living thing left behind. Dear God, I drown in You and breathe in Peace.

Metaphysical Errands

Mental Abilities

Each mental capacity we have can be redirected, regardless of how often we may have misdirected it in the past. Memory can be used to remember this moment instead of the past. Even if our current circumstances are difficult or painful, our ability to *remain* in the present offers us the opportunity to hear the voice of the Divine. Our ability to forget can be employed to release our mind from old hurts and petty lessons. Concentration can be focused on Love as easily as fear. And we can use our imagination to set for ourselves a gentle path on which to walk.

Suggestion

Imagine the type day you want. Picture the kinds of exchanges you would like, the tone of your encounters, and the mental attitude you want to hold to. Then remember this picture of light as you go about your day. Quickly forget to follow up on opportunities to condemn. Do not take offense and hold it sacred. Concentrate on your worthiness to be happy, and release your mind from arguments that you or anyone else deserves to lose. You did not make yourself. You were not your idea. There is Something more to you than shifting self-images. This Something makes you worthy of your kind attention and happy concern.

Look past your body. Steer your mind down avenues that lead to peace and to the recognition that you are an inseparable part of that which constitutes the Core of all that is eternal. You do exist. And what could possibly change that? Now is the time to face the fact that your incalculably important mind will not die. Return it to God, whose peace can give rest to a world that has waited too long in pain.

Salvation without Attack

Whenever we recognize that we are making a mistake, our ego has a plan for our salvation: Feel guilty or place the blame on someone else. But that is not a correction. If we continue making the mistake, our ego now tells us this proves we *are* our ego and that any effort to extricate ourselves is futile; therefore we should not try. It will say that our continuing in the mistake demonstrates that what we truly want is in competition with God's will. If that were correct, our situation would indeed be hopeless. However, it is not that we oppose God's will, but only that we misunderstand it. Our will and God's are the same: satisfaction without vengeance, life without abuse, and love without bounds.

Suggestion

None of your mistakes are new. They are old responses tried once again. A mistake does not add darkness; it merely continues it. It doesn't really matter how long you make a mistake or how often while making it you appear to realize your error without correcting it. All that is important is whether you are now ready to make an effort on your own behalf. Whenever you feel strong enough, lay aside the evidence of your guilt and the hopelessness of your condition, and quietly let all fear pass from your mind. Be calm a moment, then remember that the Divine could not be mistaken in what It sees in you. You are God's. You are not owned by an ego, and your body is certainly not all that you are. End your period of rest by trying a while to feel the way you imagine it would feel to be God's beloved child. If you succeed in having this sense of peace and certainty, even for an instant, you will recognize that what made the mistake is not the part of you that you wish to honor.

An Indirect Approach

Belief is made by wish. Human perception is filtered through desire. Yet how we *act* on our perception can be either direct or indirect. The means by which we clear our vision does not have to be quick or harsh. A gentle and relaxed approach to life is as valid as one that is proactive and aggressive. Because people and events are always changing, even to merely wait is at times a powerful approach to solving problems.

Suggestion

Rather than attempting a direct release of your present beliefs about this body, that car, those people, this room, there are times when it is helpful to adopt a gradual approach. Begin by asking yourself what you would *like* to believe about that phone call, this chair, those hands, about even the overall way the day or your life is going, or anything else your attention turns to. Don't assume that, because a thought or emotion is directed toward something minor, it has minor effects on you. You are seeking a mindset that simply does not condemn anything, because condemnation, even if it appears justified, can never bring peace to you, your loved ones, or the world. Imagine the way you would like to see whatever it is you notice. In this way you are taking responsibility for how you desire to see and not arguing with yourself about "how things really are." Now, it does not matter that you think you are unable to see a gentle light within this other person or in yourself, for you will begin by trying to *imagine* that you can. This would be dishonest if you were attempting to deny the nature of the ego. Or if you were a victim of the world you see, which you are not. If you perceive the innocence in others, you will be led to your own innocence. If you see others as inadequate or evil, they will function as your guide to pain. Either perception is your choice. However, one is based on fact, the other on incomplete awareness. That is why it is not dishonest to use an indirect approach if your purpose is to circumvent mental conflict. Close your eyes and ask yourself what you would wish to see if you could, and how you would feel on seeing it. Remind yourself of the splendor God has placed within every living thing, then take one person as your subject and try to recall what true loveliness is like. That ancient memory is still within you.

Forgiving

Guided Meditation

Step 1:   Think of someone you are angry at. Anyone you have found difficult at times or who brings to mind a fearful thought is an adequate subject. Take a moment to picture this person in detail: how she stands; how he dresses. Remember anything about the person's body and mannerisms that seems familiar. Now add to this image any memories of insensitivity, conceit, unfairness, cruelty, stupidity, or other unforgiving thoughts that come to mind. Notice how tight and small your mind becomes.

Step 2:   Turning your attention away from this person, recall a moment when you or someone else was thoughtful, happy, or kind. The incident does not have to involve the person in Step 1. Just think of a time when any adult, child, or animal extended love or enjoyment to another, any moment of forbearance, generosity, or humor. Notice the soft light and feeling of relaxation that come into your mind with this thought. Think of another incident and still another, until you

have within your mind a palpable sense of
light. Using the touch you would use to
communicate your tenderness and love,
shape this light into a garment. This can be a
cape or a coat or clothing of any kind. Now
gently place this garment of light over the
individual in Step 1. Allow yourself a
moment to see the soft glow that now surrounds this person.

Step 3:   As you continue to watch, see standing
behind the individual a brilliant figure of
light. You may have a name for this figure—
saint, prophet, angel, guide, Jesus, Holy
Spirit—or you may have none. But have no
doubt that this is the Divine, the One who
always comes to heal and make pure. Now
watch as this holy figure walks into this
person you have not yet forgiven. Pause a
moment to see the light of your peace that
covers the individual, and the Light of God
that fills them. Notice that they become very
still within God's presence as they feel the
release within your mind, and in their own.

Gentle Reality

Guided Meditation

You have before you a little box. It contains a new set of eyes made purely of love. You screw out your present set and screw in the new ones. For just a moment you leave your eyelids closed and think of all the distressing images your old eyes brought to you. Now you open, then quickly close, your new eyes. The light of the Universe you just saw was very bright and healing. You wish to look more fully on such a lovely sight. You slowly open your eyes again and allow all good things to come into view.

Mantra

Let all voices but Love's fall silent.
Let every thought but God's be still.
Let all faces become the Face of the Divine.
No relationship exists except God my Friend.
No memory remains but of God my Self.
There is nothing else to see.
No other Hand to hold.
No other Breath to breathe.
No other Heart to beat.
No other Life to live.

Time Has Ended

Guided Meditation

You are standing at the end of time looking back. You have merely picked out a particular series of events and focused your thoughts on them. It all seems very real indeed, and the windings of the plot you are involved in appear demanding and important. Notice, however, the rather chaotic and "fast-forward" quality of the drama. But now a stillness comes over you, as if some dear Friend has gently placed a hand on your shoulder. Softly comes this reminder: "You have only drawn an old nightmare into your mind. Nothing more. Relax your mental hold on it, and let this scene of confusion return to the dust of time." You watch the frantic tale you called your life recede. It fades as it returns to that tired old dream where all things end, and it dissolves completely from your mind. Now you are in the kingdom of God, a creation of pure joy held forever in Love. Your mind is no longer trapped in a body. You are free.

Consulting the Divine

Guided Meditation

What do you have to lose by acknowledging an experience greater than yours? Is it truly less idolatrous or doctrinaire to call a spiritual advisor on the phone or to read a book of printed truths than to consult the One who understands the road before you? Is it not clear that there is a specific Wisdom that transcends the "lessons" of our very short personal history? What could you suffer by trusting in what you have always professed to believe: that time and death do not change reality? All that our body perceives is not all there is. For one free moment, gently lay aside your arguments and your fears of appearing ridiculous and *see* if there is not Someone who waits to bless and guide you. Just be still and feel the Peace that beckons you within each situation. If you are still, you can trust your gentle inclination. There is never only one thing to do, only one option available. The plan of Peace can be found in many alternatives. The guidance of God is not an act of the body or a behavior. It is an act of the heart. Following guidance is choosing to be like the Nature of guidance. How could the leadings of Love narrow choices and restrict possibilities, when Love is boundless?

Mastery and Effort

A useful distinction can be made between mastery and effort. Our ego mind frequently points out that we have not mastered forgiveness. We thought we had forgiven someone, but the grievance or grudge keeps resurfacing. This may be true, but it is irrelevant, since our part is only to make the effort to forgive this instant. To look back and *judge* our efforts not to judge simply compounds the mistake.

Suggestion

The next time you feel defeated or confused, try thinking a thought with some degree of love in it. Any thought will do. For example, picture a gentle exchange between you and a friend. Remember something endearing your child or your pet once did. Or imagine the opposing sides in a current world conflict laying down their weapons and advancing on their former enemy in welcome and friendship. If you would rather, make your effort this way: Assume a relaxed position, close your eyes, and silently and very slowly repeat the name of God. As you do so, focus your mind on the Experience behind the word, and allow your mind to be drawn into that Experience. If you prefer mental stillness to images or words, then let your effort take that direction. Every religious, mystical, or therapeutic system in the world entails concentration in some form, so do not throw out any aspect of effort that can be of use to you, under the mistaken assumption that to remain mentally scattered is a form of acceptance. Make your effort in the way you wish, for as long as there is no distress; then go about your day without looking back to judge the results. When you feel ready, try again. Each attempt you make will cause another desirable shift in the direction of your mind. And sooner than you think, you will complete your goal of turning it right-side-up.

The One Reminder

There is one reminder we cannot make too often: *"I am not alone."* There is One who is with us even now—in *this* place and time and situation. That is why we never need do something else first. Not even one thought must we correct by ourselves. In fact, we can do nothing by ourselves. And our ego is merely our belief that we can.

Addressing Thought

We need only address God in our mind. There is really nothing else that has to be pictured or felt or spoken to. The past need not be reactivated or figures from old or recent scenes re-addressed in sharper terms. It will not make us safer to worry about the future, then lay plans to prevent what we fear. The best possible basis for decisions made in the present is not fear of the future. An insight we receive from God does not have to be repeated to someone we think needs to hear it more than we do, nor do we need to use Love's reminders to scold ourselves into being a better person.

Suggestion

Within the quietness of your thought, you can safely talk to God and God alone. Any scene you call to mind that serves to denounce your or another's motives will only waste time. It will frighten, isolate, and appear to weaken you because of the "laws" it affirms. Whenever you notice this "idle thinking," gently return your mind to something that matters. It is indeed possible to save yourself time. All attempts are beneficial, yet you can do something, one thing at least, to increase their beneficial effect for you: You can address no one but God within your mind. Speak to your Friend in your deep and silent heart, where the hush of holiness enfolds you in Peace.

Fear of Unity

Why do we resist loving certain people? Is it not because we have judged them and do not want to unite with what we believe is a distasteful reality? Even if a person's character is as we believe it to be, there is also a greater Truth in which we can have faith. It is impossible to unite with a projection, and even egos clearly seen cannot know oneness. The thing we are afraid will sully or pollute us if we love it is not what we are asked to love.

Suggestion

In the presence—actual or visualized—of this person you dislike, gently release yourself from your defensiveness. Become harmless before him or her. Become as blameless as rain falling on grass. Slowly lay down your armor and breathe away your piercing screams of impatience, fear, or anger. Quiet all thoughts of objection, however mild or great. Then open as a flower to the sun: without effort and without thought. As all defenses fall away, you will see that this child of God yearns only for what you yearn for: to be seen and appreciated and to be recognized as innocent.

Pleasant Effort

If you feel discouraged about your progress, if you want to take the next step, yet the thought of even mastering the first step tires or saddens you, know that you are mistaken about what is expected of you. Effort is to be used only as a means of letting go of effort. You simply make the effort to remember that you need do nothing. Yes, you will be firm with yourself, but only to the end of staying clear that you do not know your way Home, that you do not even know the next step to be taken, and that your strength can only come in putting yourself back into the arms of the One who carries you. The biggest hindrance to our spiritual progress is our suspicion that we are being asked to figure something out and do something other than rest in peace. Behind these fears is an assumption that the rules whereby one advances demand a sacrifice, that "nothing worth having comes easy." So we think we are being asked to do a thing that will be unpleasant, tedious, or daunting. But this is never so. The rules of advancement call for the very opposite: trust, quiet contentment, and openness.

Suggestion

It isn't possible that you could truly want to do something that would constitute a retreat from your heart's goal. If ever you think that, you have misunderstood where your treasure lies. When you feel irritated, dejected, or put upon, or when there is the sense that you are fighting yourself, do nothing. Doing nothing is all you ever need do. But you do need to do that much. Admit how little you know, then mentally step aside. Wait for God to move. We are like a child, and the Divine is like a shining train that takes us into a land of unexpected wonder and beauty. Our part is merely to allow ourselves to be carried along.

Preoccupations

Dwell only on what can be extended and shared, so that your mind may remain one. One in peace and love. One in its healing vision. Dwell not on the distressing, the conflicted, and the doubtful. Dwell not on things of smallness—little hurts and petty accomplishments. Dwell instead on a knowing look, a kindness given. Dwell on gestures of patience. Dwell on laughter and music rather than the discord of relationships. Quickly forgive others their mistakes. Do not leave your mind at war. Look beyond the small annoyances and distractions so you may continue to hear a single Voice and see a single Self. Look at that which makes you happy. Try, at least. Only a simple vision can help and heal. One that is divided has already become part of the problem it beholds. Oneness, simplicity, and kindliness are a Thought that is highly practical and effective. But choose it because it is true. Keep your interpretations fresh and still by interesting yourself in the points of Light around you. God shines through all things. Allow this recognition to come softly into your gentle mind. A single vision, a simple mind, if carried everywhere you go, is Heaven.

Touchstones

What does your mind return to for safety? What is its place of rest, the "reality" it grounds itself in whenever you feel stressed or bleak? Is it the time of day? Do you look at your watch? Is it your appearance? Do you glance at reflections or look for signs of acknowledgment? Is it some activity you have planned for the evening, or perhaps some broader consummation or life achievement? Do you find your "rest" in the thought of what you contain—your influence, your position, or your name? Do you feel secure in what you have accumulated—property or savings or a "fine" family or "good" friends? Does your mind return to some external such as these for a little reassurance that this present turmoil really doesn't matter? If so, you have not yet changed your reason for being here. Yet you can, now, if you wish. You already know that the little platforms on which you attempt to rest, whatever they may be, will eventually collapse. Because they always have. And if now you diligently build your health or desperately hold to your loved ones or strive to secure your reputation, it is only a matter of time before you see again how frail were these defenses. But you need not continue in this manner. Put your weight on something that will bear it. You will recognize what you are relying on by what your mind keeps returning to for reassurance. If it is Love, your increasing peace and confidence are assured. If it is a single thought of Beauty, you have picked wisely, and you have indeed chosen for the future and not just for a few fleeting moments. Peace is not external. It is internal. Like a pond ruffled by a passing wind, merely return again to stillness. Make peace your touchstone, your shelter, and your home. No matter how often you stumble, make this your single response: to wait in peace for your God.

Vague Guilt

It isn't possible to know the answer yet not apply it. If you have a vague feeling that you know what you should be doing, but are not doing it, you are mistaken. Your ego does not know anything, but it thinks it does. It therefore wants you to feel guilty for not applying *its* answer. But it has no answer.

Suggestion

Address directly your suspicion that you know the way out. Ask yourself what specifically are you supposed to be doing. If what you now hear is still coming from your ego, you will not be able to complete it, no matter what it is. Our ego is always doing what it does not need to be doing now, and telling itself that it should be doing what is impossible to do now. So turn from your ego and face the Light. Do not prepare yourself first. Honestly admit that you don't possess "good" judgment and that you need help. Yesterday's lessons will not work today. Turn to God because of your honest recognition that you are not clear how to respond to this, then wait in peace for the answer. Drop all demands, and especially your definition of the situation. You can't define the situation you think you are in without believing you know the problem that needs solving. And you can't believe in a problem without feeling guilty for not applying an answer, even though you don't have one. The answer *will* come, but not from the direction your ego thinks. Simply wait, and in the meantime do not judge anything. Your part is merely to resign as your own counselor. It is a small part, but essential to your freedom.

Innocence

There is no fear greater than the fear of being happy. And there is no reluctance more deeply seated than the unwillingness to see sins as mistakes. Who could honestly denounce other individuals if it were admitted that all they did was make a mistake? And who could fail to forgive if they deeply acknowledged that they found it desirable to be judgmental? A sinner is seen as internally dark, a thing unworthy of life, to be attacked and weakened. And within our censure is all the evidence we could ever want of our superiority. We mistakenly believe that our value is in how we compare to others and that to see them as innocent reflects badly on us. So we remain hard and exacting in our vigilance that no evidence of guilt go unnoticed. Yet our fear of the sinlessness of what God has created also leaves no possibility of recognizing our own purity. To have any hope of happiness, we must first recognize those times we are afraid of innocence. They are the same moments that we ourselves resist being free. Let us therefore practice genuine self-interest. Let us renounce comparisons and in their place experiment with tolerance, which is the willingness to be happy.

Beautiful Balloon

Guided Meditation

There are two perceptions of this world: one dark, the other bright; one heavy and bleak and desperate, the other abounding in life and sparkling with love and peace. One is certainly hell, the other Heaven. You have seen the world both ways, although your memory of the latter vision may seem distant. Rest a moment in peace, then imagine your mind as a beautiful and buoyant balloon. Its nature is to soar in freedom and enter Heaven effortlessly. But now it is chained to a world that is old and tired, a place where all things have grown weary with hollow victories and inevitable endings. Today it is within your power to release it and let it fly to its natural Home. It will carry you fully within it wherever it goes, for it is your mind. The chains that hold you to a barren world are all the separate things you still think meaningful, each high and low. If a thing has some private meaning for you, it binds you to a loveless perception. Fear a thing no longer, and that chain is broken. Withdraw your longing from something else, and another tie is released. What binds you comes in many forms and names, and they vary with each person: something owned or desired, power sought or lost, an imagined slight or one given, adornments, regimes of beauty or super health, past lives as proof of attainment, special gifts and abilities. Whatever seems enticing anchors you to this world, until that time you are willing to take a more honest look at just what it is you cherish. Take that time now. Review the anchors and the chains. Do not overlook your lists of personal attributes and imagined failings. Then lightly toss each of these weights off from your mind until, clean and free, you can leave the old world behind, not as something you dislike, but as a place that no longer controls you. And soar like a beautiful balloon into the light of a new and rapturous world, which is your Home and your Destiny.

Mental Projects

Decisions

When our purpose is clear, there is no question what to do. Ultimately, our progress is seen not in what we do but in what we perceive our goal to be. Either we assign our ego's objective or God's purpose, and that is determined by what we choose to consult within us each time a decision is made. It is impossible not to consult something. If we think that our past or the future is an adequate guide, we will not believe that the urgings of Love can direct us.

God's purpose cannot be surmised or rationalized. It must be experienced. We cannot merely second-guess and naively reinterpret, because those are forms of avoidance. They serve to strengthen our belief that goodness can be disguised and that what is meant to help us can be sent to us in the form of a "trial" or curse. This, of course, is nonsense, because God is fair, Love is present, and Truth is unequivocal.

Asking for guidance from our Core of peace facilitates our recognition of the loving consequence of what we do. Asking, however, is not what establishes a beneficial result. Blessing is our inheritance from God and therefore our right. It cannot be negated, but it unquestionably can be overlooked. Turning every decision over to God protects our mind from a conflicted view. The love content of our perception determines how we characterize our relationships, our health, and our sense of an abundant life.

What we turn to for counsel will not create the future, but it affects our experience of it. In this respect, our happiness comes from accepting God's direction and losing interest in the strictly personal and in our baser instincts. Since we usually operate as if our future were up to us, it is helpful in freeing the mind from fear to ask for guidance with decisions concerning the future. Begin with those anxious choices you recognize, and do not weigh their importance. Ask what you are to do. The answer may come quickly or gradually. Once you see your peaceful preference, act with confidence, then wait happily until you feel the need to ask again. Obviously you should not act until you know from what part of you you are acting.

A good general rule is not to ask what to do until the decision can be acted on in the present. To ask God prematurely is merely to request that your anxiety be relieved, and the answer you receive may do no more than that. It will not necessarily relate to the guidance you will receive later. A second rule is to never reconsider the answer—which was after all a product of faith—unless it appears that by your continuing in the decision, someone is being hurt.

It is possible for us to so weaken our ability to hear, that the answer will seem to come and go or will be felt only after we have asked more than once. But multiple requests are not necessary, and they usually add uncertainty to the process. When you act on the peaceful impulse you feel, it is the right answer, and your ability to experience guidance quickly grows as a consequence.

A third guideline is an understanding of the manner in which guidance comes to mind. It is unlikely that you will be given broad instructions about dramatic changes in your life situation. It is more likely that you will be told each step at the time it is to be taken. It is therefore helpful to remind yourself that you do not know what anything you have been told is leading to. Clearly there is no merely personal goal you could think of that would throw light on the Purpose behind your inner instructions. Be content to take each small step as it is given, knowing the time will come when you will look back and see a meaning more vast and beautiful than anything you had imagined.

A final guideline is to keep in mind that you are not seeking behavioral instructions but attitudinal healing. The Divine is not concerned with which potato you choose or which checkout line you stand in, but that you choose and stand in peace, feeling as best you can your connection to those around you.

The apparent need to decide is actually a moment of internal conflict. The mind pauses in uncertainty.

Asking for guidance is a safe way to acknowledge your Source and return your mind to peace. However, when you experience no hesitation in what you do and you feel lifted up and carried in peace, it is not necessary to ask about every detail. When you are in this state of effortlessness, those around you are usually comfortable, and certainly no one suffers from your words or behavior.

Whenever feasible, turn your moments of asking into moments of quiet listening. There is no question about what to do, and this is the only lesson we are actually learning. Our will and the will of God are in fundamental agreement. Only the ego is undecided. Only it experiences the need to question. Our purpose is to step gently around doubt and confusion and proceed in peace. If we can accomplish this through questionless listening and pure thanks, we are better off than if we believe the advice we receive is the entire Answer. So whenever circumstances allow, relinquish your assessment of the problem, drop all questions and demands, and turn directly to God. All you need say or do will flow from a pure and unconflicted peace.

We do not "create our reality" or determine the course of future events, for that would render a Plan meaningless. We could not misplace ourselves without altering the activities of everyone we encountered. If the Universe contained a single mistake, it would affect its perfect functioning throughout. Altering Reality and modifying Truth are not part of free will, yet the ego will counsel that by admitting our fallibility, we remain humble. But is it humble to claim the capacity to change Life?

We do not stand at the point of control but at the point of choice between two interpretations. We do not choose between a thousand different futures, but we do decide how we will characterize our part in the interchange among God's children. We are not in control of external events, because only by defining ourselves as something small and weak could we believe that everything is external. As a body, events surprise us. We feel vulnerable and ultimately alone. Only the *degree* to which we are "caught off guard" varies. We try to exert ourselves; we attempt to take our little lives into our own hands and to make others behave, but very quickly any sense of progress in this direction is shattered.

There is another Maker of this world. All mistakes are translated by It into precise steps toward freedom. We cannot do anything that has not been anticipated and turned into a benefit for us and those around us. But this must be seen before it will appear to function within our experience. On the level of Divine interpretation, all that is true in Heaven is true on earth. And this *can* be recognized as the way things actually operate now and here. In Heaven there is no need for decisions because All has already been given to us by God.

We do not need to concern ourselves with how we can have more, but we do need to see that we have Everything. A future would be required only to provide us with what we presently lack. But what could possibly be added to Everything? Our path is a mental shift from an illusion of needs to a Reality of wholeness.

It is as if we are reviewing what has already happened. We are taking a last look at an old and failed dream. A review does not call for choices between events but for reinterpretation of the whole. All that occurs in a dream is the same, for it remains a dream. Thus our only real choice is to continue dreaming or to awake. God comes now to wake us. It is a gentle awakening, because all we thought we did to Reality had no effect. Love remains forever Love. And you are the child God loves.

A thousand times today we will be presented with the opportunity to awake. Seeing that this opportunity always exists, we can release the future and choose only this instant. We can be content for events to unfold as they will, to let our body tell its little story, and to recognize that whatever direction life takes us in cannot affect our Reality. We choose God, which means we choose to be good. We choose straightforward love, immediate helpfulness, and true charity. Our only questions are: Am I willing to fulfill the function Love has given me this moment? Am I willing to forgive my mistakes and those made by others? Am I willing to be happy and free within this time, and through my holy Mind, bring a measure of rest to all the world?

Idle Thoughts

The body, in all its many activities, does not require the cooperation of the mind. The mind can influence the body, but the body cannot of itself call to the mind, change it, diminish it, or extinguish it.

Although our ego claims we must "think about" what we are doing, this is not entirely true. "Thinking about" is a substitute for concentration, the ego's ploy to remove our mind from our control, or at least to make us believe we have. The ego suggests that perhaps we would like to keep our mind within Love, but alas, there is a task before us that requires practical thought and no other part of our mind is available for anything else.

All things fall more easily into place when our mind is not conflicted about what we are doing—for example, if we are not wishing we were someplace else or engaged in another activity or thinking that what we are doing is really someone else's responsibility. Whenever we are inwardly relaxed, we will not be distracted. And our body will function efficiently. A chattering mind *is* distracted, whereas internal comfort allows mental focus to occur naturally.

After you have had a quiet moment with God, your ego may suggest that there is now something pragmatic you must do and all of this spiritual stuff must be laid aside so you can keep your mind "on task." If you were then to rest your mind fully on the activity before you, this would indeed be a pure form of meditation. However, when you observe closely, you see that as your body undertakes the activity, your mind is not now focused on what you are doing, but is standing back commenting on it. Then it drifts off to think about something not even indirectly related to the task. It aimlessly passes from one subject to another, apparently at random.

The terms "idle thinking," "projection," "dissociation," and "loveless thinking" are, in spiritual terms, interchangeable. They only emphasize different aspects of the same mistake. What, then, is "idle thought"? It is thought that appears to be idle or neutral, but it is not. We believe an "idle thought" remains within the head and does not go forth to influence the world we see—a "private" thought that carries no consequences. A thought that changes nothing. A thought that affects no one, and therefore is undeserving of our attention or remedy.

In fact, though, idle thinking, when it is all that consumes the mind, is a deliberate form of repair and maintenance undertaken by the ego. It systematically mends all the fences that were weakened during our moment of peace. It is anything but a neutral activity, for it reinforces the thought system on which our entire perceptual world rests. It is not harmless, because all forms of pain flow either directly or indirectly from this mental activity.

The difference between "fantasizing," "dreaming," "perceiving," and what usually passes for just plain "thinking" is the apparent length and intensity of the thoughts involved. Any other differences are imposed in retrospect. All mental activity is the same except what is within the Mind of God. The kind of thinking we are most familiar with is composed of short fantasies about the past or future. Words are indeed "heard," but words of themselves have no meaning without a mental referent or impression. Idle thinking, in whatever form taken, is an attempt to rehearse or rewrite, to plan or reactivate. It overlooks now and deals with a time that is finished or is yet to be. Very little real thought is contained in this process, because true thought is a calm seeing and is accompanied by a gentle delight throughout the whole contents of the mind. Real thought is love.

True thoughtfulness is never off on some hopeless search, as all seeking for what one does not presently have must be. It is an act of present discovering and present finding. It is simple acknowledgment of what one truly possesses. It is gratitude, the only mental activity that joins with God.

The beginning step in freeing your mind from its

useless wanderings is stillness. Stillness may be associated with physical quietness, but the effort must be made to carry mental calmness and peace into each situation the body enters, or else a block to your happiness has been left in place.

Far more moments than you may recognize at first are already provided during which it is feasible to pause and speak to God. The first broadening of stillness may therefore be the willingness to use these periods of rest or transition. The opportunities for these will appear to multiply as they are utilized. It is not a mistake to deliberately plan these moments into your daily schedule. As long as we believe in planning, we *will* exercise that belief, and it benefits us more to exercise it lovingly than fearfully.

As you try to bring goodwill into each activity, the means whereby this can be accomplished will be provided. A *search* for means is merely a delaying tactic of the ego. Your honest desire to be in Love and of Love is all you need. It isn't possible for you to want an increase in mental freedom without being shown how to obtain it. God merely waits for an open heart.

"Ask and you will receive" is an instruction for successful prayer that points to our heart, not to the Heart of God. When we discover what we truly desire, we automatically have it, for God unfailingly gives. But when we are afraid to be free of a problem, God will not do anything to increase our fear. Therefore, "be not afraid." Search gently within your heart to find what you honestly want. Seeing what you want, you will no longer be afraid.

As was stated before, we do not have to "think about" what we are doing, only seek peace in what we are doing. Words are not required in order to think. Yet words can be useful in directing the mind's eye. A single focus is used to replace the hundreds of conflicting focuses offered by the ego. The time will come when you will be able to leave your mind unguarded and it will no longer project. Yet, clearly, there are very few who have reached this level of learning. I can assure you that I have not. Nor do I know anyone personally who has. So I am merely offering you the words that have helped me begin to relinquish the need for words.

First, we only say the truth. We accept it intellectually. Then, we begin to suspect that the truth may in fact be true because of the evidence we are beginning to see in our experience. Later, we grow in fondness and trust of the truth. And finally, we recognize that we ourselves are true.

Because minds are joined, in a sense everything in our environment does the same thing at the same time. If I defend my ego, it will appear that all the egos around me defend themselves at the same instant. If I feel defensive while by myself, the figures that people my thought become defensive within my fantasies. And if I am dreaming, the figures in my dream will protect themselves, each against the other. Only the personal manifestations that the defensiveness takes will contrast. Each ego will defend itself in its own way, and these *forms* of acting out may differ widely, but at the center of each will be a knot of fear. Viewed in this way, another's behavior, whether fantasized, dreamed, or seen physically, acts as a helpful alarm that warns us that we are hurting ourselves by continuing to sustain our present attitude. And this attitude is manufactured by so-called idle thoughts.

Although a little effort is needed to keep your mind from spinning tales of limitation and attack, it is a restful effort and a more enjoyable use of the mind than the ego's version of "letting go" or "giving up." When the mind drifts into conflict, the pressure can become strong and the distress quite noticeable. Now comes the alternative of a little peace and quiet. Turn your thoughts to God and partake of Love's pleasant imagery and healing considerations. There is no limit to the number and variety of thoughts you can think that contain love. Direct your mind to this single purpose, and every point in your consciousness will relax. The world itself will be affected by your gentle choice.

Dreams

If this book is correct in its assumptions, everything discussed here can already be found in your experience. The question it attempts to raise is only whether you wish to continue experiencing everything in the same way, or can you happily release yourself from certain beliefs and "realities."

It should be clear that whatever we think is real is reflected outwardly in what we see. Yet when different "realities" are observed to conflict and refute each other, a choice will be made between differing sets of evidence because they point to opposite conclusions about what we are. A good example is in the question of what would we see if we really looked honestly inside ourselves. What do we actually want on the deepest level? Do we have a desire to heal or an impulse to hurt?

If the kingdom of God is truly within us, that same position is not occupied by evil. Yet our present way of seeing is highly conflicted. We first see darkness, then light, light, then darkness, as our basic motivation. Our vacillating perceptions keep us locked into the same tired life pattern.

As has been stated several times in this book, for everything we see there are two interpretations. These windows of perception appear to open onto opposite worlds. Looked at fearfully, people appear to be motivated quite differently than when looked at with love. The world we see instantly reflects back to us a picture of where we desire to be.

Our dreams at night are excellent illustrations of how the mind can create an entire world, then forget the part it played. The project proposed here is simply for you to practice transferring your knowledge of the dynamics of perception to new areas of experience. You will take what is clear in one part of your life—for example, what happens when you dream at night—and apply it to those times when you don't feel you are distinguishing clearly between truth and illusion. To do this, you must allow yourself to practice an assumption you may disagree with. You are not asked to believe this working premise, only to test it for yourself.

The waking state and the sleeping state, although differing in the "laws" they represent, are equally affected by our thinking. All that is seen by the body's eyes, whether the eyes of the body that moves about in a dream or those of the body that arises after a night's sleep, is subject to projection. Not a projection by the body, but a projection of the mind. This is not a difficult point to grasp, since we all recognize how dreams and fantasies are formed.

During sleep, our mind often pictures itself as a body that may be similar or dissimilar to the body that lies in bed. This dream-body does not think. The dreamer thinks for it. While we are dreaming, we usually believe that our mind is contained wholly within a particular figure we have identified with. But neither that figure nor any part of its anatomy is doing the thinking— although if, during the dream, its brain is damaged, the figure may appear to think differently.

All the figures in a dream appear to think and act independently of each other and are often surprised by each other's behavior. Yet it is still the dreamer, who lies asleep, who produces everything. If, then, we are like Adam, who fell asleep and never woke up, we form our waking experience in much the same way as we do our dreams. Assuming this is true, what else can be said of both states, and what lessons can be learned? Here are just a few:

1. There are two kinds of dream activity. One is dreaming about a world that is itself a dream and is therefore twice removed from Reality. But who has not also heard Truth speak in a dream, or at least felt for an instant a deep peace or a genuine love? One type of dreaming excludes fairness and everything that is Eternal; the other reflects what is true of our relationship with God. In a sense, our life work is to practice dreaming only dreams of forgiveness. Awakening in God cannot occur until we become proficient and consistent in this form of mental discipline.

2. Within our mind is at least the suspicion that much of what we do is for purely personal interests, that we have at one time or another misused our friends, betrayed our family, and wasted our time and talents on petty pursuits. This suspicion is certainly true of our dominant and superficial motivation. But it also goes to the question of our deeper motivation and operates as an underlying tone to all we think and do. Consequently, a sense of basic guilt is never entirely absent. It seems that no matter what we attempt, we cannot experience one unequivocal instant of release. But is this entirely true?

As in dreams, there have been at least one or two instances of release within everyone's life. At times they become so dim in memory that we wonder whether they occurred at all. Did we deceive ourselves in this as we have in so many other things? Yet they did occur. In fact, only things reflecting Truth *have* occurred.

These moments of light or pure seeing have certain characteristics that distinguish them from our usual way of perceiving. Within their gentle perspective, the past and future fade in importance, so absorbed are we in the beauty that surrounds us. Nowhere do we see a thing we cannot forgive. Our way Home is certain now, and we are content to leave all things in God's hands. Our mind stays fixated on nothing, but instead moves freely from one scene of peace to another, and the "evidence" of our guilt does not enter our awareness, because it lacks fairness and Truth.

By contrast, a loveless perception is the movie of a slow-motion temper tantrum. Everything seen holds something we don't like, and the only question is whether to reject it now or later. Nothing is left unjudged. Innocence is a matter of degree, and peace is merely the thought that someone suffers more than we. Since this way of thinking is based on comparisons, everything is seen at odds with everything else, and friends are only those with whom we feel the least competitive at the moment.

Our present experience is clearly a mixture of both a fearless perception and one that is fear-dominated. Most people are not even aware of when and how often they change perceptions. But our more immediate problem is that we become confused as to which way of seeing has value. We love a little, attack a little, and no real progress is made.

But aren't you already noticing that the differences in texture, shape, quantity, and degree within the world of form begin to diminish in importance as Beauty is perceived? Haven't there been moments when *every* detail was lovely, not just a fleeting few? When the heart was gentle and compassionate? When another's body was no longer an adequate testimonial to the person's character? When distance became irrelevant to communication? And perhaps even death faded as a block to the awareness of someone's presence?

Something within this universal undoing of limitations quietly informs us that if we could see to the end of time, we would understand everything that has occurred in our lives. This new recognition does not point to guilt; it sets us free—as it does when dreamers become aware of their responsibility for a dream. We see that we have not changed the nature of Reality and *can* change the nature of a dream.

3. Unless something that happened in a dream is thought to indicate a fact about our daily life (an assumption made in various systems of dream interpretation), anything seen as merely a dream is easily dismissed. In fact, the mind erases dreams almost as quickly as they occur. Who continues to argue with a figure in a dream once they have awakened from sleep? And who, having seen that the direction of events was merely dreamed,

continues to plan against it? In short, no one reacts to what they recognize as an illusion.

It is feasible to apply these insights to daily life. It is not that we deny the events of the world or somehow try to rationalize them, ignore them, or even understand them. Rather, we turn them over to God with the recognition that only the Divine understands their purpose. "You can forgive, but you can't forget" then becomes, "You can forgive only by forgetting." To forget does not mean that we become insensitive to pain or underestimate the effects of tragedy on ourselves or others. It simply means that we accept on faith that Peace can be brought into every situation and that God's healing consciousness can sustain us through difficulties and even personal devastation. Any form that fear takes becomes less compelling when seen in the light of Love.

4. How the mind imagines itself as something it is not is also seen in dreams. Not only is a body required—something to see and hear with—but other bodies are needed to react to it and "prove" through independent witness that it is indeed a thing set apart.

As children, many of us had imaginary playmates. Here again is a thing set up in thought to act as if it has a separate mind and will. And for as long as we saw a benefit in its remaining, it appeared to act independently of us. Any attempt we made to get rid of it strengthened our impression that it was real, because there was no real playmate to get rid of. Only our loss of interest in the purpose it served made it disappear.

An ego is very similar to an imaginary playmate. In a sense, it is an imaginary identity because it is not eternal. It is not even consistent within its own story, changing its beliefs and goals quite easily. And, like any illusion, it is strengthened when confronted directly. That is why "Do not fight yourself" is the first rule of safety. What you are fighting is your imaginary identity. Cut off its source of power and the ego fades. And that source is always our desire to keep it. When we no longer are interested in being separate, in being special or set apart in any way, but are fully occupied with Love and desirous of uniting with those around us, we will have no purpose for an ego, and so there will be none in our experience. That at least is the goal.

5. All misery is in one spot. Although there are thousands of things going on in a dream, there is only one dream. Whatever cannot learn this is also in the dream. Whatever is depressed, cruel, sad, defeated, in pain, fearful, arrogant, or

deceived is in a dream, because our imaginary identity is contained wholly within the part of our mind that projects, just as it was when we slept last night.

That is why the Answer is so simple. Wake up. But how? Decide for any component of the waking state—forgiveness, grace, happiness, tolerance, kindness, now, gentleness, love, stillness—and, to the degree your decision is sincere, you release the dreaming part of your mind from the problems it produced.

If you focus on a difficulty and consider it apart from its context, then try to solve it, you may succeed in eliminating that *form* of distress, but you will still be distressed. If, while you were dreaming that a monster was chasing you, someone gently whispered, "It's time to get up," you would remain asleep if you insisted on first escaping the monster. Do not say, "I must first change this about myself," because whatever struggles is not part of you. Instead say, "I merely need to turn from a dream and wake to my Self."

Awakening requires only our willingness to practice a single spiritual idea. It isn't necessary to understand hundreds of spiritual concepts, pore endlessly over a scripture, or attend seminars on how to awake. If anyone did no more than treat others as they would be treated, their spiritual progress would be swift and sure.

6. When I awake from sleep, I understand that all those who appeared to surround me in the dream were neither animate nor inanimate; they were simply imagined. My mind had divided itself into figures, and I had actually conversed with no one separate from myself.

The people in my dream had served the purpose of convincing me that what was external functioned independently of my wish and that I was therefore not responsible for the behavior of others, for their sins, joys, or pains. For within my dream, I had thought from inside a head, lived inside a body, and peered out through eyes at strange and unasked-for events. Nothing was my responsibility except my own protection. I was the sole provider of my happiness. If I didn't go after what I wanted, no one was going to do it for me, and whatever I did in this respect was innocent in comparison to what was occurring around me.

Yet all of that was an illusion of the dream. I was merely alone in a private fantasy. There is, however, a place where we are not alone, where whatever is seen reflects Truth accurately because it is not viewed as separate from us. In the experience of God, nothing but life can be touched. There are no bodies with sightless eyes, nor desperate minds caged inside skulls. Life does not submit to dying flesh, and "success" is not reserved for the fortunate and the few. Each and all are known as One in the embrace of Love.

Of this Truth we have but glimpses as yet. But those gentle liftings of the shroud of fear do come, and they reveal a world alive with contentment and brilliant with caring. Every time we choose simple peace in place of any aspect of a nightmare, we wake more certainly and live more fully. In God we are not alone.

7. If one were to read superficially what has been said so far about dreams, one might think this approach could result in callous treatment of other people. After all, they are just like figures in a dream. If only this half-truth were practiced, the outcome would indeed be lacking in kindness, and many there are who have fallen into this trap.

The purpose of recognizing what part of our experience is illusion is to see more clearly and respond more fully to the part that has true value. If we accord attack and love equal value, we are not in position to confer a real blessing, because we unwittingly withdraw it the moment we extend it. And this type of conflicted message does characterize what passes for communication between most people. We believe we can correct others without making them unhappy. We think we can be right without being miserable. This confusion arises from an improper distinction between dreaming and loving.

It is not that we need to neglect any aspect of other people. It is simply that we add love to our vision of others so that we are not limited to the ego's interpretation. We wake up *by* loving other people, because only love sees Love without distortion. Coolness and arrogance are not vision. A reflection of Love *can* be seen in any aspect of the world, because what is true is never absent from the part of our mind we share with God. The spiritual content of our mind is present in our perceptual world, but it is not always recognized.

Imperfect glass can appear to distort a landscape that is viewed through it. But the glass does not change the landscape. Fear is a dark and distorted glass. What are you if you are not a body? Where are you if you are not confined to this particular time and place? Perhaps these questions frighten you. Yet every aspect of ego perception has a counterpart in Truth that is pure and beautiful. Each individual has an Identity. And for every meager bodily image, for every cruel or misguided motive, for every arrogant belief, there is a gentler view already made to take its place and to deliver a healing in exchange.

Don't you want to wake up to a happier, more peaceful life? Maybe you are afraid that Truth is not an improvement on your present experience. Possibly you wish to wait a little longer to see how a special person or a certain course of events will turn out. Or is it that you are afraid of losing the little you have and possibly even your self? Perhaps it seems insensitive to turn to the peace of God when so many in the world are suffering.

A dream is only a shattered mindset. The world we see is like a broken mirror. What is reflected there is incomplete and highly distorted. Love puts the pieces back together and presents our mind with a picture that accurately reflects a healed world and therefore gladdens our heart. It is not important how this is done, but it is all-important that we want it done. "Do I want to see other people as lacking or as whole?" "Do I want to be justified, or do I want the world to have deep and lasting peace?" "Do I want small advantages or complete freedom?" "Do I want Love or fear?" Only our heart's answer to these questions controls the time of our awakening, for nothing external can hinder it.

Summary

You are asleep. Yet God, your higher Self, is awake within you and is all around you. Even in sleep you can hear what is entirely You. Therefore listen to God. Even in sleep you can feel what is already Real. Therefore awaken in God.

Communication

Strictly speaking, we do not communicate; we allow communication to be. Peace—not attempts to change, thwart, overcome, break through, or make a point— opens wide the channels of understanding and acceptance. Real communication is actually a stepping back from the effort to "get something across." It is a moment's rest from needs. This gentle contentment permits an extension of our thoughts to others through a simultaneous welcoming of theirs.

Any self-image, held rigidly in mind, interferes with natural relating. A desire to manipulate contains the thought, "This is the way you are and I want it to change." We cannot orchestrate our performance and still see clearly to whom we are speaking. Prideful announcements, calculated compliments, verbal talents used to set us apart, "kind" words motivated by guilt, attacks on third parties, controversial pronouncements, "constructive" criticisms, and questions meant to highlight another's error are not real communication because they cannot be wholly shared.

Nor does such a mindset accept with complete happiness another person's point of view. As best we can, we must permit one softly illuminated idea of equality to encompass both parties. We settle back into enjoyment and choose to be free. At the very least, we recognize that the other person doesn't owe us anything. Wholeness makes no demands.

The ego's answer to verbal conflict is to quickly provide us with grounds for being right. This may lend a temporary sense of power, but only on one side of the relationship. No sense of joining can accompany it, and the apparently larger "size" of our ego soon appears hopelessly small against the universe with which we are now at odds. If you feel a small stab of anxiety as you start to speak, you have defined another as disconnected from your self. Remember that your body does not *have* to express inequality.

Nor is mere verbal agreement the answer, because it can be, and often is, only superficial. No two egos are ever in *full* agreement. The promise of an exchange is not fulfilled if we arbitrarily adopt a different stance. Yet if all life emanates from Love, is anything truly opposed to us?

Unquestionably there appear to be many blocks and impasses, and numerous are the ones who stand in the way of our safety and happiness. But what can stand before the light if all is Light? Both perceptions of reality cannot be accurate. Our work is to choose between the two. Either we resolve to believe in innocence or we will continue cherishing guilt.

The understanding and acceptance of Love are in each of us. There is always a way of seeing that, a way to have faith that if we could view others through the eyes of the Divine, we would recognize ourselves in them. Oneness is discerning the familiar in another. Our objective is a simple one: In conversation we seek an experience, not just an intellectual exchange. We want to extend and receive enjoyment and understanding. The verbal form this takes is actually irrelevant.

To attempt correction of others is to insist that, for the moment, their faults are all there are to them. The Universe contains no mistakes, and our insistence that it does only depresses us. Instead, we focus on an exchange of love and drop the expectation that our gifts be treated with respect. We gently decline the offer to feel misunderstood or unfairly treated. Silently, we join with the spirit of the one before us, which is a part of God and therefore of our Self. We wait for the eternal communication that is always occurring to dawn on our awareness, knowing it will become apparent once we have cleared a quiet spot within us where it can be heard.

A helpful approach to communication does not differ from a practical attitude toward most other situations and conditions: Stillness works; attack does not. If you were in prayer and an angry thought crossed your mind, you would not delay your communion with God by engaging in a private analysis of it or in a long refutation. You would simply open it to the light of day and quickly turn your attention back to God. When we are with another, we are in a potential state of prayer with God. That is why we cannot hide our thoughts from ourselves and still fully connect with those around us. That doesn't mean we are "honest" to our ego's ever-changing stream of petty thoughts and attitudes. Rather we are honest to the *relationship*. Friends know what to say and not to say to each other.

You have probably had the experience of having someone described to you and upon meeting them realized that the description didn't fit. Perceptions are largely based on a state of mind, and we have all had the experience of being seen through another's perception. Even though we have changed, this person continues to see us as we once were or as they always thought we were.

We believe what we want to, but we also see what we believe. Choice operates on the level of desire. We are free to believe what is occurring in Truth, or to make for ourselves still another interpretation. Yet once the choice is made, the out-picturing of our wish is almost automatic.

When the mind appears to be engaged in idle desires, it is really exercising a particular set of beliefs. This becomes our silent affirmation of how we want our lives to be. We may, for example, fantasize mock conversations in order to produce the feeling that our positions are right. Being "right" is the gift offered us by the ego to turn from trust to distrust, from Oneness to separation. But in this turning we also turn from God and from our Self.

One way to deal with this type of mental misactivity is to ask, "What do I *want* to believe about my current relationships?" Because what we believe is what we experience. Do we *want* a life of confrontations? Do we *want* new opportunities for personal vindication? Our own selected replays of past incidents and our imagined future ones affirm that we do. Recognizing that we have chosen mistakenly, we choose again. This time we release others from their role as victimizers and our role as victim. And we can make the same choice in the middle of a present confrontation. We simply rest from defensiveness. We stop characterizing another's motives and function, knowing that God alone assigns each one's role. Instead, we allow a blessing to settle over all we see and every word we hear. And we wait in Love for a new appreciation of the conversation to be given us.

Because we recognize that we perceive a relationship as a problem, our first step is to undo the order we have imposed on the components of the relationship. How we have set things up must be relinquished before we will find ourselves in a position to see the parts arranged differently. The way we have others classified prevents a solution to the difficulties between us. So we forego our descriptions and acknowledge that it would be better if we were wrong. Turning to God, we say in all honesty that we are unable to instruct ourselves how to respond to this person, then we listen for Love's gentle Answer. We will always hear the Answer when we become as quiet as the Answer Itself.

The rule for successful communication is to attempt to share only ideas that can be peacefully received by others. Once it is recognized that nothing is accomplished by attempting to correct another, our ego frequently retreats to a new position: "I am willing to forgive them, but they continue to judge everything *I* do." The suggestion here is that somehow the other person should pick up on what we are attempting and do the same.

It is as simple to forgive unforgiveness as it is any other mistake. You *have* this person's *deeper* cooperation, and the miracle that awaits you depends on this truth. You and I are not special because we know a few spiritual concepts. We are equal with everyone in the eyes of God and have been given limitless freedom. Yet simply knowing what needs to be done is meaningless unless we do it.

We will never gain another's undivided external cooperation, because for us to see someone as external is to believe that their interests cannot be identical to ours. The solution is to stop fighting that appearance, no matter what form it takes, and mentally seek out the deeper Self within them. If there is a Place of Stillness in us, the same is in everyone. Love recognizes its own. Love sees a common set of interests because it looks beyond behavior, beyond past personal history, and into the urges for goodness that unite us with others from within. Even if there is no apparent change in the relationship, we have silently called to the presence of Love within the other person. That affirms the Truth, and one day they will answer our call.

The brilliance of God does shine. It is the light left on for us in the dark. It is our welcome Home. There is one Friend in all our friends. This is the gentle assurance we look for. We deceive ourselves whenever we focus only on an improvement in the outward situation. Seek no confirmation except an increased sense of God's presence. And this is always received quietly. It comes with our wish for peace, held lovingly in thought and extended to all. We are engaged in putting ourselves back together. Our sight has been shattered, but not the fact of our Oneness. Each person we encounter appears to hold a lost piece of us. It joins with us the instant it is recognized. And love is the way to see it.

Special Areas of Practice

Money

Our finances and our livelihood are areas that we often keep separate from our faith, as if Love should not be consulted about such worldly affairs. Consequently, these areas frequently generate anxiety and conflict in our lives. Anything that makes us feel more separate and vulnerable will create fear, and when we act from fear, fear always accompanies the outcome and will take form in our lives in some way.

We cannot hold tightly to a sense of personal ownership and control and still have a mind that is open, happy, and welcoming. Nor can we merely turn control over to another person and find freedom by denying responsibility. We are responsible for everything, because everything is potentially an act of worship.

Either God can be trusted with our needs or not. God is not reliable *sometimes*. Erratic trustworthiness is meaningless. To first decide what we want, then look to God as the means to get it, is arrogant and spiritually meaningless. In God alone we recognize both our true need and its Answer. We are directed in all things, but the Divine cannot be used to eliminate the anxiety we feel when our faith is tentative.

God can plan for our happiness and provide for our safety. But have we demonstrated an equal ability? Love is our food and shelter, not merely the means of obtaining them, and in this recognition are all temporary needs met. To seek safety in having more money or possessions, or to pride ourselves on having little, keeps us attached to the hopeless process of trading one form of emptiness for another.

The number of things we own or the number of years we live does not attest to our spiritual advancement any more than scarcity or recklessness add meaning and significance to the body that experiences them. Only by relinquishing our small and bitter authority will we awake in Love and know the freedom that comes from trust. Nothing less than All will ever satisfy us.

Possibly this much can be safely generalized about money:

> No one should be denied our help because they cannot pay.

> And we should be equally as open to giving money as to receiving it.

> We should not spend money out of fear or make our priority in life to save money. Our aim is to be guided by Love.

> God cannot be "bothered" by too small a question. But to use the mind to acquire or to believe that the Divine rewards us with money for

thinking the right thoughts are clearly not forms of surrender or worship.

Quitting our job is not an act of faith. Having to borrow, scrounge, and mooch off others is not more spiritual than working. A job can be as holy an activity as we want to make it. Faith is exercised inwardly and is not an outward gesture or appearance.

Neither wealth nor poverty should be sought to enhance our self-image. *All* self-images are of the ego.

Obtaining money should never become our priority. That limited a goal will not heal us or make us happy. By making connection with the Divine our purpose, we discover how safe it is to leave the future in God's hands.

Sex

The deep yearning we sometimes feel for a physical relationship has within it a yearning that is deeper still.

We are not at home in a body, and we are not fully and unwaveringly wanted by any other body. Nor do we find anyone physically perfect in all respects. Even the most devoted parent is thankful for changes in their infant's height, weight, and the like.

Anyone can wear out their welcome, and everyone needs their private moments. Yet we do have a Family and a Home, and in that Place the welcome is endless and without conflict. Perhaps it is that Connection for which we yearn within the symbolism of sex.

Passion is longing, and longing does not lead to peace. There is nothing wrong with desire, but it is obviously not a quiet sense of present wholeness. If we think we are lacking anything, the impulse to obtain it merely reflects a deeper thirst for Everything. We can yearn for the kingdom of God even though we already have it. Although we may mistakenly interpret a spiritual impulse as being physical, that mistake is not a sin. And it isn't necessarily the most helpful approach to fight the symptoms of that mistake.

The need for sex and the means we use to pursue that need are not the same. The belief that we have to meet a need destructively is the fault of the belief, not the need. Yet God can show us a new use for every means we now employ. We are not asked never to value the body—even Divine guidance is gentle and caring of each person's body—but we are asked to see the body in ways that will allow us to be happy.

Our present approach to sex may call for deprivation on our part or sacrifice from another, and that is not necessary. The desire to have what we think we don't have will make us feel less than whole. So in our heart, if not our body, we need desire only what we already have, which is a Bounty without limit.

We all tend to treat our body as something apart from our mind. It often seems that the body has goals that conflict with mental goals. Our mind may fight the body's impulses and desires, often with little or no effect except the feeling of losing control and adding residual guilt. The solution to conflict is always to step away mentally from conflict, not to think there is some way for a split mind to conquer itself. A mind that is at peace will extend its peace to the body. A mind based in God will be harmonious, and the actions of the body that represents that mind will be kind. Kind to itself and kind to others.

One should not, on philosophical grounds, attempt to eliminate an outward form of relating that has become common to a relationship. For example, one should not insist on abstinence from sexual intercourse with one's spouse under the assumption that abstinence is more spiritual.

Conversely, one should not attempt to pressure another into having sex, or into beginning a new form of sexual practice. Pressure in general is the primary cause of relationship failure, just as acceptance is the key to sustained love. How frequently two people have sex indicates nothing about the strength of their relationship. And how infrequently individuals express themselves sensually does not trumpet their moral superiority.

The mere actions of a body are not what is spiritual. Fighting against any aspect of a behavior we have identified with will not of itself lessen that identification. Actually, that approach tends to keep us narrowly focused and confines our life experience to inadequate pleasures and short-lived gratifications. Nor can the habit of fixating on limitation be solved through endless examination and analysis. Only Light gives light. We cannot produce it by ourselves, because light is the recognition that we are not by ourselves.

The longing for other bodies is grounded in the deeply held belief that we are solitary and not an extension of Love. Therefore be gentle with yourself, for gentleness is of God. In that attitude of kindliness and true helpfulness, Love will come to you and lead you past sexual problems and a thousand other hindrances you did not recognize, all at the same instant.

Children

Each stage of development our children enter is another opportunity to respond to the part of them that will not change. Only the Eternal can be related to, communicated with, and joined in full cooperation.

Our ego will argue that a "new" child calls for still another definition of ourselves as parents. If we adjust by merely changing our self-image, we will still perceive our interests as different from our child's, and we will have ample evidence of opposing minds, wills, emotions, and conflicting rights to time and property. We cannot think that our role as parent gives us power over our child and expect to have the experience of one Self.

We make a central mistake in any relationship that becomes a problem. We deceive ourselves that we are encountering a thing that is not like us. This applies whether we are dealing with city hall or "the terrible twos." The final answer does not lie in isolating one aspect of the situation and trying to force a change. When relating to children, our goal remains to enter into the realm of peace just beyond the picture perceived by our senses. And nothing short of this entry brings us the rest needed to make peaceful decisions.

Whenever feasible, our initial response to a child's unexpected behavior should be inner stillness and

openness. Only an instant is needed. This practice reha-
bituates the mind. The old reactions of anger and fear
are turned from in preference for the experience of connection. A still and loving mind will not feel at a loss,
nor will it be cruel.

The way Home for both our children and ourselves
is invitation through attraction. It is a path of gifts leading to the final Gift. The experience of Heaven begins
with "yes." "No" merely marks the places where happiness cannot be found. "No" is a temporary, and sometimes necessary, expedient, but it is not a sufficient
communication to lead us or our child safely forward.
Once our children understand that we mean "no," that
we understand it and live it ourselves, they accept it
as their own answer.

"No" is not properly a warning of our intention to
attack. It is a firm, safe, unmovable buffer against what
will hurt someone who has the understanding of a
child. As parents, we allow our children to come up
against it, until, in their own time, they realize the
buffer will not move. However, they must also realize
that *we* are not what will hurt them. That is why it is not
necessary to intensify the factors they are afraid of in
order to change their behavior.

Our goal as parents is not to modify behavior but
to deepen connection. We don't know what our children
will become or should become. They belong to God,

and their destiny is in God's hands. We honor and respect them as their holy guardians. We tend Heaven's garden, but we don't know what seeds are planted there.

We are not against our children, and therefore never do we teach them fear through intimidation, scolding, shaming, or any other form of withholding love. We teach safety through harmlessness. How could anything but Love be safe?

As parents, we are consistent in our deep connection to our child. There is no virtue or practicality in consistency of rules we thought up at some moment in the past. Our child is present; God's wisdom is present; and our capacity to see our child's state and what needs to be done *this time* is also present.

At times our consistency seems to take the form of out-enduring our children. This approach is an improvement on anger, but it is improved further if we can transform endurance into gentle, changeless patience. As loving parents, we are content to wait, remaining firm but not dangerous, until, if need be, our children change their minds. Our "no" is now a safe enclosure, a form of watching over them.

Never allow the question to become "What am I going to do about it if my child defies me?" Our objective as parents is not to defend our pride. That merely teaches pride. Nor is our goal to communicate dislike or disapproval. Scissors, knives, matches, and other things young children don't understand must be taken away even though they may scream their misinterpretation of our intention. But older children do not have to be put in pain or banished from their favorite place in order to "pay" for what they have done. Punishment ("consequences") is not an aspect of Love. We do not need more tools to guide our children than God needs to guide us.

A simple "Do only this" is easier for small children to understand than abstract explanations of what they should not do because of how it might endanger them. Teach approach, not avoidance. Teach love, not fear. Teach simplicity and clarity. Allow your thoughts and actions to fit what your child *is*, and do not do anything out of fear of what your child may become. Show your children their unchanging Source of reward, not a thousand shifting shadows.

By how you live your life, give one clear instruction that will never fail to guide your children safely and happily. It is not words we teach or learn; it is an experience. Therefore, enfold your children in your experience of generosity, of release, of gentle perspective, and of sweet lightheartedness, until at last you see their interests as yours, and yours as theirs, and only Love as the Parent of us all.

Marriage

The marriage ceremony symbolizes a preexistent State. Oneness is recognized, not invented. This State cannot be destroyed, but it can be forgotten. The ceremony itself is one of many ancient symbols. It celebrates the happy, eternal fact of the unity of all life and the exclusion of none. In marrying, those who are one acknowledge their Oneness.

The spiritual reality of marriage does not have to be worked at. Correctly seen, marriage need only continue unresisted. But our perception of what marriage symbolizes does have to be protected, nurtured, and tended. In a sense, God gives us a beautiful garden, but we have a penchant for sowing weeds.

Our "work" is to give continuing welcome to all the seemingly scattered evidences of Oneness. It is to keep the garden whole and good. We can distort our perception of its beauty, but it remains pristine. Likewise, we can never truly separate ourselves from another child of God.

Relationships of various kinds are perhaps our most accessible means of experiencing the Divine. God is loved and honored through the children of God. The times we set aside for prayer and meditation would appear to be our best opportunities to commune with the Divine, but if these are too closely associated with physical isolation or are mere exercises in superiority, we fail to experience our deep connection with others. Few, however, can miss seeing that the function of marriage is to lay aside isolation and inequality and to join as one.

As the light of Truth begins to dawn in thought, we may suddenly have the mystical experience of seeing another as our self. This makes no sense on a perceptual level, but it makes perfect sense on the level of Love. Now there is no boundary to our prayers, for we see that we have nothing to lose from another's gain.

However, the level on which only egos encounter can be depressing and fearful. As this is seen more honestly, a marriage may appear to become increasingly dark. To those consciously attempting to wake in Love, this melting of the candy shell that covers some forms of destructiveness can be very distressing and may be misinterpreted as personal failure.

There are two steps in seeing the light within our partner. What is dark must be recognized as without light or value, and light must be seen as harmless and desirable. No compromise is possible, for to continue accommodating abuse or darkness in any form is to want another experience besides love. Couples who make any problem more important than their friendship will instantly lose sight of the light of oneness.

If confrontation is valued, love will appear to be a

highly unstable component of the relationship. In your communications, emphasize no thought within you except your desire to increase the friendship between you. Ask yourself, "Will these words (this act, my attitude, this position) promote oneness, or will it promote separation?"

Only through connection can you remain open to healing, and unless you are open, you *will* try to hurt your partner to protect what you believe must remain secret. Therefore, hold no part of you separate. Cherish no private assessments. Be transparent and harmless. And if this remains your goal, the two of you can join hands and walk past any difficulty.

As stated before, openness is a function of the heart, not of the mouth. Saying just anything to our partner or confessing what we know will shatter and devastate the one we love is not loyalty or devotion and is certainly not kind. If we are ever to know love without limits, there can be no range to our giving. To want something from another is to utterly misunderstand their role in our happiness. Another person is our opportunity to extend what we *are*.

Other bodies are not our means of proving we are incomplete, burdened, or in need. That is why attempts to negotiate sometimes set in place a deterrent to free communication and peaceful relating. Negotiating can be of temporary help and is preferable to friction, but if just one partner forgives completely and replaces their own anxiety and criticisms with goodwill, they become the governing factor in the relationship.

Being able to talk about things and to formulate a mutual approach to difficulties is clearly desirable. But it is not necessary to pressure our spouse to talk about what we judge to be wrong with the marriage. It is not necessary to urge our spouse to take responsibility for their part or to confess their mistakes. It is not necessary to force compromises or even to formulate rigid plans for dealing with a recurring problem. Nothing is really necessary except that we remind ourselves alone that we are not in this relationship by accident and that all that occurs *can* be seen in love.

A kind vision is always a possibility. It will occur when one person pauses long enough to recall their heartfelt gratitude for the crucial role their partner plays in their spiritual growth, whether their partner intends this effect or not.

Because all minds are in communication, one happy, forgiving, restful thought will of itself extend throughout all areas of a marriage. Nothing exists that can actually stand in the way of this expansion. To accept full responsibility for everything and guilt for nothing is true humility and the sure road to a successful marriage.

Healing

Sickness often makes us feel alone and vulnerable. Our mind, which should be a source of comfort and release, clings tightly to fear and conflict. An illness, particularly a serious one, can make us believe that somehow we failed or that we are being punished. Perhaps we think, "Why did this disease pick me out from so many people far more deserving of this sickness?"

Yet disease is never a reason for self-censure or shame, any more than "good" health is our personal accomplishment. In a world of sickness, who can avoid being sick? As the saying goes, "No one dies in good health."

We are truly healthy only when we allow our minds to return to an innocent and peaceful way of seeing. Healing is thus completely natural. Once again, our mind functions as it was meant to. In all we think and see, we are whole and free.

Since illness is unavoidable, the most we can hope for is to remain healthy for longer periods than the "norm." All things live off the death of something else; that is the way of the world. And if illness is defined as physical distress and limitation, instead of the very arbitrary way most people think of it, everyone is sick most of the time. This can be a very freeing recognition of a useless battle that need not be waged.

Special Areas of Practice

Yet it is also possible to look honestly at any difficulty and recognize that it holds nothing we want. If that is seen unequivocally, physical healing often occurs. But if that degree of honesty is not possible at the moment, there are ways to build within us a greater love of freedom.

Disease usually engenders fear, so to release the mind of fear is to return to the only real health we can have on this earth. Following a strict policy of foregoing all medicine and other external means of healing often increases fear rather than reduces it. Such a decision should not be made without the aid of internal guidance. God's peace within the moment is a better consultant than the memory of an old position we may have outgrown. Love is always a *present* help during difficult times and simply does not have an agenda about the "correct" way to treat an illness.

If you feel guided by Love to try a mental approach to healing your own body, your chances of success will be increased if you continue to remain open to any assistance, whether medical, "natural," or "alternative," that your inner Physician suggests. Only God heals, and only the mind is ever truly healed. Clearly one mind can overwhelm another mind, but the delusion that we have personal healing powers, or have been singled out by God for special divine gifts, can delay our way Home more than a period of pain.

Just as death is not a defeat, a body that returns to health is not a testament to spiritual superiority. Positive physical change, without an accompanying release from fear, has little significance spiritually. It is neither good nor bad. Love is the only miracle, and our part is to have faith in the way that Love expresses itself in our life.

Healing Imageries

As in all things, we protect our mind from self-deception when we turn to God for instructions on how to proceed, and it is helpful not to have preconceived ideas about any course of action. I have known individuals who were healed through traditional medicine, touching, mental imagery, silent "treatments," physical repositioning, colors, fragrances, breathwork, herbs, sounds, special machines, placebos, diet, and movement. Open your heart, allow God to tell you what to do now, and trust the Answer.

Relinquishment

Turning our problems over to God heals because what the mind does not hold, it cannot manifest or project.

Think of your body as a teaching aid. It is like a screen on which your thoughts are pictured. If you have failed to forgive yourself or someone else, this attack will be symbolically manifested in some form of physical distress. Step back from your body and pretend to attack it in the exact manner necessary to produce the distress, and perhaps you will see more clearly what you are angry about. Anger is not your ally, and it is certainly not a form of humility. Now step back again. This time you are the light of God that blesses and purifies. Gently shine away each hurt and tension in your mind and body. This is your part to play. By merely attempting this, you make the effort to bless that God has asked you to make, and you leave the results up to Love.

Stillness

Stillness heals because only a volatile mind generates fear and distress. Stillness is not an absence of sound but the presence of peace.

> Nothing is more substantive than peace, and so you can rub this deep hush of God's presence into every patch of soreness or hate. Feel the balm of peace remove completely what never really touched the child God made out of Love itself.

> Float a blanket of God's quiet snow over every form of fear. Watch the areas of trauma relax and heal beneath the soft and luminous mantle of the Divine.

Pour onto the damaged parts of your body a healing oil. Let it settle there like silence and spread like the gift of grace.

See floating down from Heaven a lovely white parachute. It carries a silver container of celestial paint marked "The Glory of God." Dip the attached brush into the rapturous golden liquid and softly spread it over each area of difficulty, until the entire landscape of your mind and body relaxes in peace.

Blessing

Giving our blessing heals, for we can always give what we have received in full. We can bless our body, which represents our present concept of ourselves, far more effortlessly than we can curse it or fear it.

Both color and music are ancient means of healing. Imagine your wounds and ailments as the sound or color you like the least. Using either the color or sound you like most, change the present tone to one of harmony. For instance, imagine gray turning into blue or honking turning into jazz. As the transformation occurs, see complete healing accompany it.

An angel of God has handed you a lantern. Direct the strong light of benediction into any place you see fearful shadows or picture dark images. As Love's radiance focuses on the troubled spot, notice that, there, your body is made whole.

Imagine that you are holding in your hand some sacred object. Touch each place of pain or deterioration with the holy object and watch that place instantly heal.

Draw a circle of light around you. Fill in every shadow and all the empty spaces with light of equal brilliance. Now switch yourself on and see that *you* are the light of this circle. Then draw your circle around the world, and acknowledge that you are also the light of the world. Behold its brilliance arching above you and the splendor of its beauty below and all about. Rest in this vision for a long healing moment. The Truth allows no hurt to remain in anyone.

Entering the Place of God

Your home and God's are one, and in God's home there is no pain.

Travel to a spot where you would love to be—any kind of place you wish to picture. Smell its perfumes and hear its gentle sounds. Leave all forms of fear behind, and watch for a while only the surroundings you enjoy. Now comes your special Guardian. This happy sight is very familiar. You knew it well when you were a little child. This One is once again answering your call and brings the healing touch you requested. Now the hand of Love is gently placed where you direct. It heals whatever bothers you there. Your relief is all that this One requests, for your wholeness blesses the world.

Forgiveness

The root meaning of the word *forgive* is to release, to give back, to let go. Forgiveness heals because it permits all forms of attack and abuse to pass from thought. This process can be quietly pictured, as well as verbalized.

> Because God wants you to be happy, you can present to God no greater gift than one of your sorrows. Picture God waiting patiently for you to ask for help. Each time you notice anything physically or emotionally distressing, wrap it as a present and hold it out to God. Watch as Love takes it and shines it all away. Now feel the deep thanks of the Divine that you have allowed your burden to be lightened.

> Breathe your pains, your misgivings, and all your foreboding into a balloon or into a giant

bubble of bubble gum. When it is full and buoyant, release it into the heavens and feel all your upset and distress transported far, far away.

Step into the soft flow of a sacred river, and allow the healing waters to wash over you and dissolve whatever distresses you within or without. With only what God made of you left behind, see how you sparkle, clean and pure, the object of endless Love. Or if you prefer a waterfall, it is there before you now, heavenly in its beauty. It pours like love from the Heart of God. Stand for a while in its gentle downpour and allow your worries and fears to wash away. Each tiny aspect of you is cleaned and healed throughout, and now you emerge in total newness, brilliant in your harmlessness toward everyone.

Summary

Changing the body should never become a goal that substitutes for true healing. Healing is merely peace, and it occurs wholly within our mind. The above suggestions are meant only to bring light to your mind. A consistently restful and comforting approach to mental change reflects the same throughout your body and relationships, and in all aspects of your life. Make your imagery games as happy and free of conflict as God's power Itself. You do not have to fight anything. You *are* Love. Picture what delights and relaxes you, and hear only what lifts you to joy. Sing a quiet song to your mind that transforms each strain of sadness you identify. Dance your thoughts to its music, and let there be dirges no more.

Honesty

To the ego, there appears to be a conflict between the intention to be harmless and the goal of honesty. However, honesty is not complete as long as certain contents of the mind are emphasized. A peaceful mind is at rest with all its parts. Gentleness responds to everything equally because it responds to everything fully. To fear no exposure of any kind is to become instantly harmless.

Forget what you have judged is needed and let yourself say what you say. How can you be certain of the outcome of your words? Therefore, forget words and wish well instead. If the world would do only this one thing—hide nothing—there would be peace between people forevermore.

It is such a relief to be open. Yet this relief is not gained by trying to make our personality and behavior so perfect that not a thing remains to embarrass us. Embarrassments are not important. As long as we retain an ego, it will attack our motives and judge against the body that acted as their agent. There is little real love, and consequently no freedom, within an ego. Only by consistently hiding nothing from God and from ourselves do we eventually relinquish the ego, because it is merely our wish to remain hidden and apart.

Hold back no part of you and you will not attack.

Openness does not contain the need to rehearse in advance what is to be said or done. If we are truly open, our words will not hurt, shame, or intimidate. Openness makes empathy automatic, and honesty is just another name for generosity. Truly open individuals do not utter every negative thought their egos conjure up. Genuine honesty comes from the heart we share with God.

It may not be apparent at first that the desire to analyze another's motives and deliver a "just" response is dishonest and secretive. Yet this much should be obvious: Love is being concealed and avoided. When no attempt is made to rank in importance one's emotions and thoughts, the contents of the mind merge, and light is the residual. All forms of darkness are merely shadow feelings. They contain nothing that cannot be turned over to God. Honesty is the coming of Truth, which dispels without effort and without attack that which is not true. The Truth, in whatever gentle form it takes, is your Friend. Trust it. Open to God; open to yourself; and through that unblocked passage, the bounty of Love will be given and received.

Letting Go

The existence of now gains credence as we journey toward it. More and more frequently, it breaks into consciousness. Gradually we come to trust it as we would trust a friend of perfect faithfulness. And whenever it is chosen over absentmindedness, for an instant the perceptual world fades, and all we ever wanted is seen to be at hand. Yet when we look at all there is to be done, we cannot help feeling defeated before we even begin. How can we use the body harmlessly at all times? How can we look at others without recalling their past actions and holding these limitations against them? How can we free our minds of fear? How can we stop valuing others for their specialness alone? The answer is we cannot meet any of these goals in the days to come. To forgive another for all time seems impossible, but to forgive them for just one instant—this instant—is fully within our capability. Whenever we release our mind from a condemnatory train of thought and allow it to return to gentleness, we are practicing pure forgiveness. To rest from judgment is to absolve from guilt. We all can direct our thoughts to Love for one moment. It is true that the very next moment we may again yield to temptation. But that will not really matter, because it will not truly be the "next" moment. It will always remain now, and now will still be the lesson we are learning. "Am I willing to love, to forgive, to bless, to heal for just one instant?" is a question that addresses itself to Reality. "How will I be able to do this tomorrow?" questions a person who is not here and a time that is not now. Say instead, "I am here. I am only now. God is all that is happening. I let go of everything that never was. And never can be."

A Benediction

You stand at the Source looking out. You are blessed, and you can extend an endless blessing. Close your eyes and imagine this happy scene of healing. You are a stream that has begun to flow in an old and dry bed. You are a bearer of cool water to earth that is parched and dead. In your wake, seeds sprout up and bloom. The earth turns to life at your coming. From this time on, you may offer a cup of cool water to everyone you meet or think about, to those yet to come, and to those who have been here and gone. You may offer it in joy and ask nothing in payment. You need not preach or exhort. You need not ignore or disdain. You may safely offer all you have so that you may have still more of its Source, of which you are a part. You offer a simple choice, an alternative to cynicism and despair. And because you stand in God, you see all things in God's light. Nothing before you deserves to suffer. No one is unworthy of help. You extend Love's light to an earth that turns willingly to receive it. You stand in God. You stand in Love. You offer light to shine away the cold shadows of fear. You offer, but you do not manipulate or force. You stand in God, and you feel Love's gratitude pour through you with each one who accepts God's gifts. Resolve to remain as constant in your giving as is your Source, until that time comes when every living thing will wake to its innocence and find itself at Home.

About the Author

Hugh Prather is the author of nineteen books including the best-selling *Notes to Myself, How to Live in the World and Still Be Happy, The Little Book of Letting Go*, and *Standing on My Head*. He lives with Gayle, his wife and coauthor of thirty-nine years, in Tucson, Arizona, where for many years they were resident ministers at St. Francis in the Foothills United Methodist Church. Hugh is also the host of Everyday Wisdom with Hugh Prather on Wisdom Radio and Sirius Satellite Radio. Hugh and Gayle have three sons and a dog that thinks she's a cat.

To Our Readers

Conari Press, an imprint of Red Wheel/Weiser, publishes books on topics ranging from spirituality, personal growth, and relationships to women's issues, parenting, and social issues. Our mission is to publish quality books that will make a difference in people's lives—how we feel about ourselves and how we relate to one another. We value integrity, compassion, and receptivity, both in the books we publish and in the way we do business.

Our readers are our most important resource, and we value your input, suggestions, and ideas about what you would like to see published. Please feel free to contact us, to request our latest book catalog, or to be added to our mailing list.

Conari Press
An imprint of Red Wheel/Weiser, LLC
P.O. Box 612
York Beach, ME 03910-0612
www.conari.com